Baba Hanumān-ji

Jai Si yā Rām Jai   Jai Ha nu mān   Jai Si yā

Rām Jai   Jai Ha nu mān   Jai Si yā Rām   Jai

Jai Ha nu mān   Jai Si yā Rām Jai   Jai   Ha nu mān

Ha re Rām a Rām a Rām Sī tā Rām a Rām a Rām Ha re

Baba Sītā Ram

PRAISE FOR *CHANTS OF A LIFETIME*

"Krishna Das offers a gift of love—this candid, lively, and helpful guide to the path that opens the heart. Chants of a Lifetime is an instant spiritual classic."

— **Daniel Goleman**, the author of *Emotional Intelligence*

"In Chants of a Lifetime, Krishna Das opens a door to a world of boundless love. This is a book about a real and transformational path—including all of life's challenges, inspiration, and uncertainty. It serves as an invitation to unwavering happiness."

— **Sharon Salzberg**, the author of *Lovingkindness: The Revolutionary Art of Happiness*

"Knowing the sweet power and depth of Krishna Das's singing, I was delighted to see, in this honest testament, how he got there. This book shows how Kirtan (singing the names of God) enters into our spiritual heart and then lights it up."

— **Ram Dass**, the author of *Be Here Now*

"Like a night of ecstatic chanting, this book throws open the doors of the heart. Krishna Das writes like he sings: with earthy, quirky, luminous clarity. Chants of a Lifetime is a reminder that simply uttering any of the many names of the Beloved has the power to free us from ourselves, and make of our hearts an offering to the One. May we never again forget. May we never stop singing."

— **Mirabai Starr**, the author of new translations of John of the Cross and Teresa of Avila

All love

KD

CHANTS
OF A
LIFETIME

OTHER TITLES BY KRISHNA DAS

Flow of Grace (book-with-CD), 2007

Heart As Wide As the World (CD), 2010

Heart Full of Soul (2-CD set), 2008

Gathering in the Light (CD), 2007

All One (CD), 2005

Greatest Hits of the Kali Yuga (CD/DVD set), 2004

One Life at a Time (DVD), 2004/2000

Door of Faith (CD), 2003

A Drop of the Ocean (CD), 2003

Pilgrim of the Heart (3-CD set), 2001

Breath of the Heart (CD), 2001

Live . . . on Earth (For a Limited Time Only) (2-CD set), 2000

Pilgrim Heart (CD), 1998

One Track Heart (CD), 1996

All of these titles are available at **krishnadas.com**

CHANTS
OF A
LIFETIME

SEARCHING FOR A HEART OF GOLD

KRISHNA DAS

HAY HOUSE, INC.
Carlsbad, California • New York City
London • Sydney • Johannesburg
Vancouver • Hong Kong • New Delhi

Published and distributed in the United States by: Hay House, Inc.: www.hayhouse
.com • *Published and distributed in Australia by:* Hay House Australia Pty. Ltd.:
www.hayhouse.com.au • *Published and distributed in the United Kingdom by:*
Hay House UK, Ltd.: www.hayhouse.co.uk • *Published and distributed in the
Republic of South Africa by:* Hay House SA (Pty), Ltd.: www.hayhouse.co.za •
Distributed in Canada by: Raincoast: www.raincoast.com • *Published in India
by:* Hay House Publishers India: www.hayhouse.co.in

Design: Jami Goddess
Interior photos/images: Courtesy of the author, except where indicated

Library of Congress Cataloging-in-Publication Data

Das, Krishna.
  Chants of a lifetime : searching for a heart of gold / Krishna Das.
     p. cm.
  ISBN 978-1-4019-2022-7 (hardcover : alk. paper) 1. Das, Krishna, 1947-
2. Singers. 3. Music--Philosophy and aesthetics. I. Title.
  ML420.D158A3 2010
  782.3'45--dc22
                                    2009032081

ISBN: 978-1-4019-2022-7

13 12 11 10 4 3 2 1
1st edition, February 2010

Printed in The United States of America

CONTENTS

Sri Neem Karoli Baba—Ocean of Compassion, Abode of Grace.
(Courtesy of Balaram Das.)

This book is an offering to my guru, Neem Karoli Baba,
The One Love living in the hearts of all beings.

To Sri Siddhi Ma,
The full moon of devotion,
Shining brightly through the dark night of my soul.

To Ram Dass, my elder guru-brother,
through whom I first met Maharaj-ji.
In Sri Ram's own words, "I can never repay
the debt I owe to this monkey!"

To all of the old devotees from whom I learned so much about love.

To all saints and sages, of all spiritual traditions.

To all of the pilgrims on the Path of Love.

To Kainchi, my home in the hills.

Sri Siddhi Ma—the Full Moon of Pure Devotion. *(Courtesy of Jaya Prasada.)*

Guru and disciple, 1971. *(Courtesy of Chaitanya.)*

PREFACE

After almost three years of living in India in the presence of my guru, Neem Karoli Baba, he asked me to return to America. Sitting in front of him, at what would turn out to be the last time I saw him, I was petrified. When I left the States, I had given everything away, even my jeans. I imagined that I would always stay in India. Now I was being sent back. *Where will I go? What will I do?* I wondered in a panic. I didn't want to ask him what I should do when I got there, but I suddenly blurted out in anguish, "Maharaj-ji! How can I serve you in America?"

Maharaj-ji looked at me with mock disgust and said, "What? If you ask how you should serve, then it is no longer service. Do what you want."

This threw my mind into turmoil. Maharaj-ji laughed and said, "So, how will you serve me?" My mind was blank.

It was time for me to leave. I got up and walked across the courtyard. I looked back at him from a distance and bowed. As I did, I inwardly heard my voice coming from the depth of my heart, saying:

"I will sing to you in America."

INTRODUCTION

When I met my guru, Neem Karoli Baba (also known as Maharaj-ji), I met a love that had no end, no beginning. It was completely new, yet it was as if I'd suddenly found myself awake again after a long sleep. There was nothing I had to do to get this love. It was always shining, whether I was turned toward it or not. When my own negative stuff closed me down and made it impossible for me to feel that love, some word, look, or gesture of his would turn all the lights back on at once . . . and I was home again. This happened over and over, day after day, during the time I spent with him.

After spending two-and-a-half years in India with him, Maharaj-ji sent me back to the States. Then something unexpected happened. He died. I couldn't believe it! This was not the way it was supposed to be. I went into shock. Being with him physically was the only thing that had ever "worked" for me—the only thing that had ever lifted my heart out of its sadness. I was alone. I would never be with him again. I crashed horribly, absolutely convinced that I had lost my only chance to be happy. I died inside and lived with the belief that I would never find that love again. The shadows in my heart that had been hidden in the bright noonday sun of his love emerged to push me around and run me ragged, making me more and more depressed and leading me into many dark places, inside and out.

For 20 years I was unable to sing to him with real devotion. When I chanted, usually with a group of the Western devotees I knew from India, it was like rubbing salt in a wound. I missed Maharaj-ji and being with him, but the tears I cried were ones of self-pity and frustration, not love.

It was as if I'd been riding on a train, and one day that train stopped at a station. Looking out the window, I saw Maharaj-ji sitting there, and I ran off the train to be with him, leaving everything behind. When he left his body, I found myself back on that same train. All of my sadness, longing, and confusion; all of my conflicting desires, my self-hatred, the shadows in my heart—everything I'd left on the train when I met him—were still there. The one difference was his presence; even so, my connection with that presence was buried underneath all of my stuff, and I struggled to feel it. It was as if my train had entered a long, dark tunnel of self-destructive behavior and despair. All of this I would have to face in order to reconnect with him.

Maharaj-ji had sent me back to America in the spring of 1973 because, as he said, "You have attachment there." I knew it was true. I had reached a point where I couldn't absorb any more, and I had many unresolved desires that were pulling me in different directions.

Many years passed. Then one day in 1994, I was deeply struck by the realization that the only way I could clean out the dark places in my heart was to chant with people—people who did not know me from the old India days. I wanted to be in that presence, in that love, again, and I could see that what was keeping me out of that presence were those closed-up places in my own heart. It was a very powerful moment, and as much as I wanted to deny it, I couldn't. I was drowning, and it was the only rope being thrown to me. I was sure I wouldn't get another one. I *knew* beyond any doubt that if I didn't chant, I'd never find that place of love again. That place was inside of me somewhere. And I couldn't use Maharaj-ji's physical presence to open it up anymore—his body wasn't there. I had to find it in myself, and the only way open to me was through chanting.

I had to force myself to do something about it. I called the Jivamukti Yoga Center in downtown New York City and introduced myself as a devotee of Neem Karoli Baba. I said that I used to chant to him in India and asked if it would be okay if I came down and led some chanting at the center. Every Monday they had a small gathering, or *satsang,* of 10 to 15 of their students, when they read from holy books and discussed spiritual topics. The next Monday I arrived at the center and met David Life and Sharon Gannon, the co-founders of Jivamukti. They let me sing for about a half hour at the beginning of the evening. After the satsang, they said that I could come whenever I wanted. So whenever I was in New York on a Monday night, I went there to chant.

A few months later, I arrived to find that Sharon and David had gone to India. I sang for about two hours and continued doing so until they returned. When I came to Jivamukti after they had gotten back, their pillows were set up in front of the room next to mine. We talked for a while and then I started to sing . . . and I kept on singing! When I realized that I'd been singing longer than I used to when they were there, I opened my eyes and glanced over to see if it was okay. They looked at each other, smiled, and shrugged as if to say, "Go for it!"

I haven't stopped yet.

Chanting in Montreal, 2009. *(Courtesy of Liam Maloney.)*

Heading Toward the Heart of Gold

My life has been spent searching. Even before I knew what I was looking for, everything that has happened to me has led me into the presence of love, whether it was the physical presence of my guru or the presence of love deep within my own heart. No matter what my life may look like from the outside, on the inside it is a constant process of turning toward *that place,* of trying to come face-to-face with love.

> *The minute I heard my first love story*
> *I started looking for you, not knowing*
> *how blind that was.*
>
> *Lovers don't finally meet somewhere.*
> *They're in each other all along.*

— Rumi[1]

It is said that the heart is like a mirror that reflects our deepest being. If the mirror is covered with dust, the reflection is not clear. The mirror of the heart is covered with the dust of our "stuff": selfish desires, anger, greed, shame, fear, and attachment. As we let go of these, our inner beauty begins to radiate and shine.

The more I chant and share my path with seekers from so many different countries and cultures, the more I am being transformed myself. The purpose of this book is to illuminate the part of my path that surrounds and gives life to the chanting. I hope that by sharing the way I see my life, some of my experiences and some of the things I've learned while waiting for the door of my heart to swing open may be of help to those of you who are trying to open that same door.

Chanting alone is not my path. It is my main practice, but my *life*—and everything in it—is my path. I had the opportunity to spend several years in the presence of my guru, and I've been able to meet many saints, yogis, lamas, and instructors from different spiritual traditions. Without the blessing of these wonderful teachers and my experiences with them, I wouldn't have been able to pass through the darkness and despair that have often filled my life, and finally begun to learn how to be good to myself.

When we do *kirtan,* the practice of what in India is called "chanting the Divine Name" over the course of a few hours, we are letting go of our "stories" and offering ourselves into the moment over and over again. Chanting is a way of deepening the moment, of deepening our connection with ourselves, the world around us, and other beings. The Sanskrit chants that we sing—recognized for millennia as the Names of God—come from a place deep within each of us, so they have the power to draw us back within. If we go deep enough, we will all arrive at the same place, our deepest Being.

I use quite a few Sanskrit and Hindi words in this book, some of which have made their way into our American vocabulary—such as *yoga, karma,* and *guru*—and others for which I've given brief explanations. (I've also included a glossary of these terms at the back of the book.) And I've broken down my story into two parts: Part I, The Journey to India, is about waking up and beginning the search for my deepest Being and finding it outside of myself in my guru; Part II, Bringing It All Back Home, is about finding that love inside myself. It's not a hard-and-fast division, but more of a general theme throughout these pages—that on the spiritual path we turn from seeking outside ourselves for what we want in life and begin to discover the inner beauty and connection we already possess.

When you hear my story, maybe it will resonate in your heart because, even though all of us walk our different paths and live our different lives, we are all headed to the same place: our One Heart of Gold.

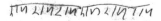

PART I

The Journey to India

My first photo of Maharaj-ji. *(Courtesy of S. Bhakta.)*

HOME BASE

[handwritten Sanskrit/Devanagari-style script]

Chanting brings me into the space of love within, which to me is my guru, Neem Karoli Baba. From the outside, he was a little old man wrapped in a blanket in whose presence I felt unconditionally loved. On the inside, there was (and is) nothing in him that wasn't love. I have to talk about my guru because everything I have that is of true, lasting value comes from my relationship with him. I'm not trying to sell him to you. There is no group to join; we already joined it. It's called "the human race." Maharaj-ji, who was beyond any sectarian beliefs, said over and over again that we're all part of one family and that the same blood runs through our veins.

"Guru" is a hard concept for most Westerners to grasp, but very simply, the guru is whoever or whatever removes the darkness from our being. For me, the guru is love—the space I enter when I chant. That space can be called anything: God, soul, presence, vastness, awareness. To me, it is *guru*.

The guru is the *living presence in our own hearts*. That presence and love might show up in our lives in different ways. Whenever it does show up, it is very powerful, because for a moment we see a flash of our own beauty. We see ourselves through the eyes of love. Whenever Maharaj-ji looked at me, I would have to look down; I couldn't bear that much love. Now I look for his eyes everywhere. For me, even after he left his body, he lives as the loving, vast, all-embracing presence in which everything exists. He is the all-encompassing sky that holds the earth, the stars, the clouds, *and* the pollution. There's no place outside of Maharaj-ji for me.

You could call this presence God, too, but the bottom line is that I don't really relate to that word. It kind of tenses me up. Growing up in the West, "God" was always something outside of me, something distant and fierce. I could never relate to what people called "God." In Hindi and Sanskrit, there are a million names of God, and they all mean God. But they're softer and sweeter, and they embody different qualities of love and give our hearts room to embrace and be embraced in many different ways.

Even so, it's not about the *concept* of God for me. The path is about love; it's about being connected, feeling that presence, and being in that love. That's the place I sing to. And that place is always here because it's not outside—it's inside. So all I have to do is remember to look for it and move into it.

MAKING THE CONNECTION

ĦⅩ ㄅ⟋ᕼ

Many of us who came of age in the '60s wanted to change the world, a task that was not as easy as we then dreamed it might be. Instead, we found that we had to change ourselves first.

The Vietnam War was going on during the years before I went to India, and my life could have been very different. After I'd quit college for the second time, I was drafted. I'd been going to see a shrink because I was depressed and had been on and off antidepressants. The psychiatrist wrote a note for me to take to the draft board—I figured that they wouldn't want me, but I still had to go to the intake center so that the Army could test me. The protocol was that first you peed into a cup, and then you had a hearing test. I sat across from a tester who handed me a pair of headphones and said, "When you hear a sound, raise your hand and touch the earpiece that the sound is in. Then lower your hand when it stops. Do it again and again as you hear the sounds."

I put on the headphones and closed my eyes. Almost immediately I heard a sound in my left ear and touched that ear. It ended and I brought my hand down. Then I heard a sound in my right ear. I touched that ear. Before that sound ended, I heard a sound in my left ear, so I touched that one as well. Then I heard more sounds.

So I was raising and lowering my hands pretty quickly. It was hard to keep up. Then I glanced over at the guy, and he was just sitting there staring at me. He hadn't even started the test! He looked through my paperwork, saw the note from the shrink, and that was that. The Army rejected me.

The message was clear: "We're not going to let you kill anyone— you're crazy."

I don't know if I was in fact crazy, but I'd always been searching for a way out of my life as it had been going so far. I had my first powerful experience of a way out in the summer before my senior year in high school, when a friend and I took peyote together. As the drug began to take effect, I looked around and thought, *Oh my God. Now I understand. This is the way it is.* Everything became perfectly clear; and I saw that my closed-up, hard, cranky, neurotic, depressed state was totally unnecessary, totally wrong. I was filled with bliss. Of course, I was also driving around with "one hand waving free" and my head in the sky and almost drove into the pond by the library! Although the lights went out again at the end of the trip, I'd seen something that I could never forget. The problem then became: *How can I get back there?*

At the beginning of my sophomore year in college, I scored ten capsules of very pure LSD. I split the first one, which was 1,000 micrograms, with a friend, and took the next nine by myself. As the chemical took effect, I'd be propelled immediately into the world of "play." It was like being a kid again and not having a worry in the world. The heaviness of my personality was gone, replaced by a lightness of being that I had never known.

On one trip I was lying in my bed, totally lost in blissful visions, when far out in the distance (the inner distance) I felt something coming toward me from the horizon. Even though I couldn't see anything, the feeling kept getting stronger. Then I saw it coming—like a wave, ready to crash over me: *A thought! Oh noooooooo!* Then I was *thinking* again. After a while I felt the thoughts slipping away from me. *Oh no! Don't go!* Then thinking left me and I was back in bliss. After some time, I felt something coming toward me again from the distance. *Oh no!* Crash! I was thinking again. This kept happening faster and faster until the space between thoughts had completely disappeared and I was just a flow of thoughts—"myself" again.

Okay, so maybe I *am* a little crazy!

Who "I" was began to change. When I took that first tab of acid, I was in college and going to classes. I had a job and played on the basketball team. By the time I took the tenth tab, I was living alone in the mountains of Pennsylvania, taking care of a broken-down farm with two dogs, a cat, two goats, and a horse, with no human beings in sight. There really was nothing to do up at the farm except sit around and make sure that the coal furnace didn't go out. If it did, I'd freeze for 24 hours until the house got warm again. Being up there on my own taught me a lot. And it was an incredibly beautiful setting. Every evening I'd wrap myself in a warm blanket, sit in a rocking chair on the porch with my feet up on the railing, and watch the sun set over the mountains. Although I was fragmented from the drugs and all of the stuff that had been going on in my life, out there on the farm, the pieces slowly started coming back together.

Late at night, when the local airwaves quieted down, I could tune in to WNEW from New York City on my little transistor radio and listen to rock 'n' roll all night long. It was the winter of 1967–68, and Scott Muni and a few other DJs were starting to play "album rock." It was a wonderful time. Although I was lonely and unhappy, I was safe. People made me crazy; I couldn't handle being around too many of them. I felt exposed and fragile. I couldn't stand anyone wanting anything from me. Up on the farm, I felt free of those worries and free of the burden of having to be anybody for anyone. I read *Autobiography of a Yogi* and let my hair grow.

The next fall I transferred to the State University of New York (SUNY) New Paltz because I'd decided to study Indian philosophy at the new Asian Studies Institute there. But when I met the director of the program, I was so disappointed and disillusioned by his manner that I quit right away. He'd rudely dismissed all of my spiritual interests, naïve as they were, so I was once again lost with no direction. I started driving a school bus for the local junior- and senior-high-school kids. They called me the hippie bus driver and we had a great time, but otherwise I was experiencing a deep depression. Then my girlfriend slept with a friend of hers who was going off to become a monk in some religious sect, and I sank into a *really* deep hole.

In the winter of 1968, the two Jungian acidhead mountain climbers who owned the farm that I was living on heard that Richard Alpert had recently returned from India with the name Ram Dass, meaning "servant of God." Ram Dass had been a Harvard psychology professor and, along with Timothy Leary, had been fired for experimenting with LSD with his students. He'd gone to India and met Maharaj-ji, which completely changed his whole life. Ram Dass was now living on his father's estate in New Hampshire, and my friends were going up to see him. They asked me if I wanted to come along, but I said that I wasn't interested in meeting any American yogis. I only wanted the *real* thing.

Off they went. They were supposed to come back the following day, but they didn't come back for three days. I remember the moment they returned. I had just finished milking the two goats— Alice Bailey and Madame Blavatsky—when I saw their old green Jaguar sedan making its way across the dirt road that cut through the field in front of the house. The car pulled around and one of my friends got out, and I swear that light was shooting out of him. He gave me a look of total, insane, wild joy. As I ran back to my house to get my stuff, I yelled, "Write down the directions. I'm leaving now!"

There was no thought involved; it was a total hit. I drove straight up to New Hampshire, taking all night because my old Volvo wouldn't go very fast. It was windy and snowing, and it was so cold that the heater wouldn't even work. There was a hole in the muffler, so the car was really loud, too. Finally, in the morning I pulled up into a beautiful long driveway surrounded by snow-covered woods and turned off the engine. I stepped out of the car into complete silence. My heart literally skipped a beat, as if it had been touched by an unseen hand.

I walked up to the house and knocked. A guy with a big beard opened the door with a funny grin on his face. He smiled and pointed up the stairs. I thought, *Ah hell, this place is too weird. I should get outta here.* But I walked up the stairs and into the room where Ram Dass was sitting on a mattress on the floor. He was dressed in a long white robe and was wearing lots of beads. The moment I walked into the room, something happened inside of me. Immediately, instantly, without a word being spoken, I *knew* that whatever it was I was looking for—and I didn't know *what* it was—was absolutely real. In every molecule of my being, I knew that *it* existed in the world and that it could be found. I didn't know if I could find it, but this moment changed my life.

Up until then, everything I knew about spiritual life came from books. I'd read *The Gospel of Ramakrishna, Zen and Japanese Culture,* and *Autobiography of a Yogi* and hung on their every word, yet in my heart I didn't know if what I was reading was really true. After all, they were only books. I was doing hatha yoga and trying to meditate, but walking into the room with Ram Dass made what I'd read real. Without a doubt, my heart knew that there was something to live for.

He motioned for me to sit down in front of him and said, "We're going to play a game."

"Oh?" I replied. What I was really thinking was, *Uh-oh.*

"We're going to look in each other's eyes." (*Oooohhhh?*) "Anything that comes to mind that you don't want to say . . . say."

Yeah, right!

We sat for about five or six hours, staring into each other's eyes. I'd never done that with anyone, and it was a very powerful experience. Of course, I didn't say the real stuff I didn't want to say, but I did become very aware of it. At some point, Ram Dass gave me a mantra to repeat. Then he looked at his watch and noted, "It's time to get ready for supper. If you'd like to stay, you can stay. Otherwise, if you're going to go, you should go now."

I said, "Thank you," and thought *I am gone!* I had to get back home to drive the school bus. I knew that I was going to have to drive the entire night to make it back in time to pick the kids up. So I answered, "Unfortunately, I've got to go."

"You're going to go? Well, don't worry, your mantra will protect you." *Hmm. Another weird thing he said. This whole thing is weird.*

I got in my car and started driving. I hadn't slept at all the night before, and after about an hour, I got so tired that I couldn't keep my eyes open. I pulled over to the side of the road and took out my old Baby Ben alarm clock. I wound it, set it, put it on the dashboard, leaned back in the driver's seat, and went to sleep. The next thing I knew, I woke up. I had no idea where I was or what I was doing. All of sudden I realized, *Oh shit! I'm driving!* I'd woken up to realize that I was driving down the right side of the road, not going too fast. The next thought that came into my head was: *Your mantra will protect you.* I screamed that mantra every inch of the road back down to New York.

A new life was beginning.

For a brief moment, the lights had come on again and I'd seen that there was a way, a path . . . that *it* was real. It made my longing for *that* a million times more intense. It also got me more depressed because now I knew that it existed and that I didn't have it. My life got better . . . and it got worse. It got better because I understood that what I was seeking was real. It got worse because I knew that I had to find it and didn't know how to do that.

All I knew was that Ram Dass had it, and I wanted it.

With Ram Dass [left] on the lake in Nainital, 1971. *(Courtesy of Rameshwar Das.)*

11

A Dream Come True

$$\overrightarrow{\text{几} \, \text{勿} \, \text{与} \, \text{勿}}$$

I finally had something to live for. I'd found there was a path that existed in the world. It existed right here, where I was. Although I didn't know it at the time, my whole way of living began to change.

After meeting Ram Dass, I kept going back to New Hampshire to see him. I wanted to be with him as often as possible because what I felt when I was with him was something I'd never felt before. I was very scared that I'd lose this new connection, so nothing was going to stop me from getting up to his place. *Nothing.* This was one time when my stubbornness was a really useful quality.

That spring of 1969, Ram Dass came down to New York and did two weeks in a row of nighttime gatherings at a place called the Sculpture Studio on the Upper East Side of Manhattan. Every day after dropping the school bus off, I'd get into my car and speed down to the city. I'd walk in as Ram Dass was beginning to sing some Indian song, accompanying himself on an Indian instrument. The room would be full; the only place to sit tended to be right up front, at the side of the stage. I'd sit with my back against the wall and immediately check out, going completely unconscious. After two or three hours of silence and talking—

of which I didn't hear one single word—he'd begin to sing again as the gathering ended, and I'd wake up. This happened every night without fail. By the end of that two-week period, I felt like my insides had been completely rewired.

It was right after this period that I had an amazing dream. Up to this time, I'd only seen a few black-and-white photos of Maharaj-ji that Ram Dass had on his wall. In my dream, I came into the gymnasium of my elementary school. At one end was a stage where the students put on plays. On the stage, I saw Maharaj-ji lying on a wooden bed, and there was a man standing behind him, dressed in a white *dhoti* (a man's garment made by wrapping a very long piece of cloth around the waist) and black vest. I walked to the middle of the gym floor and did *danda pranam*—bowing flat out, lying on the floor with my arms extended toward Maharaj-ji. As I was lying there, I kept thinking, over and over again, *Please let me feel something. I have to feel something.* Maharaj-ji got up and walked over to me. He placed his hand on the back of my head. As I gradually calmed down, bliss began to run through my whole body like molten light. It got stronger and stronger, until finally I felt as if I were going to explode. At that very instant, he took his hand off my head, and I woke up in ecstasy.

A photo of Maharaj-ji [left] and Dada just as they appeared in my dream, before I actually met them in person. *(Courtesy of Raghvindra Das.)*

A year and a half later I was in India, staying in a town in the foothills of the Himalayas near Maharaj-ji's Kainchi temple. One day I came late to the temple and saw Maharaj-ji walking alone across the courtyard. The other devotees and I had always been called into a room where he was sitting to be with him, so this was the first time I'd ever seen him walking. It totally blew my mind. He was moving in the exact same way that he'd walked in my dream: like a young child bouncing from leg to leg, almost as if he were about to lose his balance.

Maharaj-ji stopped in the middle of the courtyard and looked at me. I don't remember moving, but I found myself standing right in front of him, staring openmouthed and holding the apples I'd brought to give him. He cracked up laughing, took the apples from my hands, and threw them to people standing nearby. I stood there for a long time, thrilled and amazed—he really *had* come to see me, even before I met him physically! (And the man in the dhoti turned out to be my very dear friend Dada . . . he also met me spiritually before doing so physically.)

ॎ୳ ੮ਾਖ਼ਟ਼ਿਆਁਖੈਗ਼ ੮ਾਂਖੈ ੮ਾ੮੪

After the Sculpture Studio series, Ram Dass invited me to come and work for his father during that summer. I was overjoyed! I packed up all of my worldly possessions, along with my cat and two dogs, in my old Volvo and took off. On the way I stopped at Stony Brook, where I'd gone to college, for a Jimi Hendrix concert. After the concert, I was hanging around with my friends backstage when the manager of the rock 'n' roll band I'd sung with for a very short time came up and told me that they needed someone who could sing in the studio. All of the music was completed except for the vocals, so he asked if I wanted to cut the vocal tracks. There was a tour arranged as well. I was being offered a chance to fulfill my biggest desire in life up to that point!

Music has always been a very big thing for me. When I was a kid, I'd fake being sick so that I could stay home from school and hear the Top 40 countdown on WINS NY Radio. As a teenager, I discovered Mississippi Delta blues, and by the age of 19 I was walking around like a black 80-year-old bluesman from the South. My heroes were Mississippi John Hurt, Robert Johnson, Skip James, and the young white blues singer John Hammond, whom I tried to morph into.

My friends and I also used to listen to Bob Dylan's records like they were the holy gospel. We looked around at our parents and the world of the 1950s and couldn't find anything to relate to. It was Dylan who spread the news of a new way to live, on both a social and a political level. He also began to describe a journey through previously uncharted regions of the heart and mind. He was moving through inner space, revealing and describing a path to freedom beyond the programming of childhood. His music turned me within, and I began to discover a radically different way of living. He opened up the vision, but I couldn't find the tools to enter into it. That would have to wait until much later.

I wanted to be a singer so bad. I'd played folk music and blues at small clubs and parties, but I wasn't stable enough to really be successful. Now here it was—my chance to be a rock star! The opportunity to live the dream was being handed to me. I had to make a decision: I could follow my dreams, or I could follow my heart and go to New Hampshire with Ram Dass. For the first time in my life I felt like I'd found something with Ram Dass, and my heart was beginning to come alive with the anticipation of entering more deeply onto the spiritual path.

I'd wanted fame and rock 'n' roll more than anything in my whole life up until I met Ram Dass. I'd imagined that it would make me feel a certain way. The reality is that if I had gotten any fame, power, or money at that time of my life, I absolutely would have destroyed myself with it. The way I see it is that Maharaj-ji, whom I hadn't met yet, was watching over me and saved me from a very dangerous situation. I marvel when I see that through his grace he's fulfilling those old desires, now that having those things won't destroy me. He's even letting me be a *chanting* rock star, without having to jump around onstage; I sing sitting down cross-legged! Another difference is that instead of singing to serve my ego, now I'm singing to save my heart.

Bluesman, 1965. *(Courtesy of S. Kagel.)*

THE JOURNEY TO LOVE

Before Ram Dass came back to America from India in 1968, Maharaj-ji told him, "Don't talk about me!" Ram Dass couldn't help but talk about him nonstop, but he never mentioned his full name, who he was, or where he lived, so he felt that he was obeying the spirit of the law. *Maharaj* means great king, but in India it's used for everyone from saints to *chai wallas* (tea sellers) to passersby in the street. So there was no way of finding out whom Ram Dass was talking about.

After hanging around with Ram Dass for about a year and half, I knew that I had to go to India to be with Maharaj-ji. When I told Ram Dass, he said, "Well, look, I can't just send you to Maharaj-ji, because I'm not supposed to be talking about him. But I'll give you the address of one of his old devotees, K.K. [Krishna Kumar] Sah, and you can write to him."

I wrote to K.K., telling him that I was a student of Ram Dass's and wanted to come to India to meet Maharaj-ji. After a few weeks, I got a letter back saying that Maharaj-ji was not in the hills (K.K. lived up in the mountains), but when he returned, K.K. would bring my letter to him and ask for instructions. This was exciting—just the fact that I got a letter from India was amazing to me.

K.K. and Ram Dass were very close. Maharaj-ji had sent Ram Dass to K.K.'s house for food and instructed K.K. to help him, so K.K. felt that it was his duty to serve Ram Dass by helping me. About a month later, I received another letter from K.K. that said:

> Sri Maharaj-ji has returned to the hills, and after some days I was able to go see him at his temple. As you know, Sri Maharaj-ji does not show any kind of enthusiasm or sentiment in calling the devotees to him. However, if you happen to be visiting India and come here, you can have his darshan [sight] as so many do, day in and day out. Baba has an open door for all without any distinction of rich or poor, believer or nonbeliever, etc. It all depends on the sincerity, devotion, and earnestness of an aspirant. As you are so keen to see him, now it is up to you to decide yourself to come and have his darshan.

K.K. Sah, 2006.
(Courtesy of Rameshwar Das.)

Copy

OM   RAM
·ji·

Naini Tal.
25th. April 1970.

Dear Jeff Kagel,

I am writing to you with reference to my previous letter of 31st. March '70.

Shri Maharaj Ji has arrived here at Kainchi and we hope he will be here for the next one or two months more. Earlier he was here on the 1st of this month for only two days and then left.

I have read your letter to him and also, the feelings of the other members of the 'Satsang' have been brought to his esteemed notice.

I hope Baba Ram Dass must have told you that about Shri Maharaj Ji, who does not show any kind of enthusiasm or sentiment in calling the devotees to him, and — personalities like him would not commit themselves to anything — so it would not be advisable to make the journey specially and specifically for this purpose only. However, if you happen to be visiting India, and come here, — you can have his 'Darshan' as so many do day-in and day-out. — Baba has an open door for all without any distinction of the rich or poor, believer or non-believer etc.......... And it all depends on the sincerity, devotion and earnestness of an aspirant. I have written to other members of the Spiritual-family 'Satsangees' also.

— As you are so keen to see him, now it is upto you to decide yourself — to come and have his Darshan.

With all good wishes.

To:—
JEFF KAGEL
36 DEEP DALE PKWY
ROSLYN HTS, NEW YORK
11577.

Yours
krishna k. Shah
(KRISHNA KUMAR SHAH)

(Posted on 25.4.70).

'et भौं et भौं भौं भौं et et,
et gऔर et gऔर gऔर gऔर et et ॥'

HARE RAM HARE RAM   RAM RAM HARE HARE
HARE KRISHNA HARE KRISHNA   KRISHNA KRISHNA HARE HARE.'

K.K.'s letter to me, 1970. *(Courtesy of Nina Rao.)*

Fantastic! I'm on my way! All right, I'm going! I get to see him! Unbelievable!

Many years later, K.K. and I were sitting together at his house. He asked, "Did I ever tell you what really happened that day?"

I said, "No, what do you mean?"

You've got to understand how this worked. K.K. grew up in Maharaj-ji's lap. From the time K.K. was eight years old, Maharaj-ji had been coming to his house, because he was his father's guru. K.K. would sit in Maharaj-ji's lap and play with him as if he were his grandfather. He had an intimate, sweet, and loving connection with him without the restrained formality of a guru-disciple relationship . . . and besides that, K.K. was a spoiled brat. If Maharaj-ji would tell him to stand up, K.K. would sit down. If he told K.K. to go away, he would stay. If he said to stay, K.K. would go. It was all the play of love, and the sweetness of their relationship has continued. So K.K. took my letter to the temple, along with two others that had come from other Westerners. He entered the room where Maharaj-ji was sitting and put the letters down on the cot. Maharaj-ji was talking to the other people in the room, so K.K. sat down in front of him and began peeling an apple to cut up and feed to him (Maharaj-ji only had a few teeth). While he was talking and eating the apple slices, Maharaj-ji noticed the letters and asked, "What's this?"

"They're letters from Ram Dass's students. They want to come see you."

"*No!* Tell them not to come. What do I have to do with this?" And he went back to his conversation.

K.K. began to sulk, and he stopped feeding the apple to Maharaj-ji. Maharaj-ji noticed K.K. pouting and looking down at the floor. He pushed on K.K.'s forehead to lift up his head, and in a very sweet voice asked, "What's the matter?" K.K. wouldn't even look at him. This happened three or four times, and K.K. still wouldn't feed him the apple. Finally, Maharaj-ji said, "All right, tell them what you want."

My whole *life* was dangling on this little thread: "Tell them what you want." If it had been a different devotee when Maharaj-ji said this, I would have gotten a letter saying, "Don't come. Goodbye." But because it was K.K., everything was different. Being a good devotee, K.K. wouldn't lie, but he also wanted to serve his friend Ram Dass. And because of the way he phrased the letter, I had no clue as to what Maharaj-ji had actually said.

In Nainital, two hours before seeing Maharaj-ji for the first time. *(Courtesy of Jagganath Das.)*

When I first arrived in India, the moment my foot touched the ground on the runway of the Bombay airport, I was overwhelmed by the feeling of being home for the first time in my life! I realized that I'd never felt like that before, not in any place I'd ever lived, not even in the house I'd grown up in. On September 16, 1970, two friends and I arrived in Nainital, up in the foothills of the

Himalayas. We asked around for K.K. Sah but were told that he'd gone to Kainchi, so we took a taxi to the temple, a half-hour ride away. As the old Ambassador taxi labored up hills and coasted down on bald tires, we saw the white buildings of Kainchi nestled in the valley below. A thrill ran through my body, and I kept hearing *I'm home, I'm home* running through my head.

My friends and I walked down the steps onto a bridge spanning the narrow river that separates the temple from the road. It felt as if we were entering heaven. We stopped on the bridge and did danda pranam, extending our arms toward the temple. We entered the temple and asked for K.K. He was sitting with Maharaj-ji and told him, "They have come." Maharaj-ji said, "Feed them," and sent us some bananas. K.K. took this as a sign that Maharaj-ji was pleased with us. We were given huge piles of *puris* (deep-fried bread) and spiced fried potatoes. It was the most unforgettable meal I have ever eaten.

When we finished, K.K. took us to meet Maharaj-ji, who was sitting on his *takhat* (wooden platform) wrapped in a plaid blanket. I'd been dreaming about this moment for the last year and a half, and now it was here. I was actually seeing him with my own eyes! My friends and I had only seen old black-and-white photos, so it was unbelievable to see him moving around, in full color, and to hear him speak! The atmosphere was filled with incredible sweetness. His voice was soft and intimate yet seemed to come from far away, as if he were seeing us and our whole lives in that very moment. A thrill ran through me as I bowed to him for the first time in this life. I put the apples I'd brought next to him on the takhat. He immediately took the apples and threw them to the other people in the room. I was shocked, thinking that he wasn't accepting my offering. He looked at me and asked, "Is it right to give it all away at once?"

I hesitated and then replied, "I don't know."

"The *prasad* [anything, usually edible, that's first offered to a deity or holy person and then distributed to others] comes from God and goes back to God. When you have union with God, you don't need anything." I looked up at him, confused. He continued,

"When you have God, you don't have any more desires." Now *that* was clear!

He then asked, "Have you studied Buddhism and yoga? Do you smoke hashish? Is there any place in America that is peaceful like this place? Are you married?" Then he looked at K.K. and said, "These boys have good *samskaras* [the influence on our lives of our past actions] and come from good families. I am very pleased with them."

K.K. replied, "Won't you do something for them?" Out of his love, K.K. was asking Maharaj-ji to give us some kind of special blessing. "You know you can do what you want."

Maharaj-ji just smiled. "Why do you want this?"

"It is my duty. Ram Dass sent them."

"Is that your desire, then?"

"Yes, it is my special prayer."

"Okay, I'll do something when the time comes."

We were then sent back to Nainital and told to return in three days. I was filled with rapture. I'd been accepted into the family of devotees by Maharaj-ji! I could leave the old unhappy me behind. I was breathing new air, the air that spiritual seekers had breathed for thousands of years on their way up to the high Himalayas to disappear in search of the Great Mystery. Now I was one of them.

ुम ८/म्र ।म म्रिं ८/म् ८/म

My two friends and I settled in at the Evelyn Hotel, which was run by K.K.'s cousins M.L. Sah and S.L. Sah, both devotees of Maharaj-ji. I felt as if I were living in heaven. Nainital is a town that surrounds an ancient crater lake like a golden setting around a radiant jewel. I wandered around town in a dream. Everything was familiar: the way people talked and moved, the smells of food and the diesel fuel of the buses. Every few days, Maharaj-ji would let us spend the day at Kainchi. The rest of time we walked, read, ate, and met with his devotees in Nainital.

One night as I was walking around the lake, I became totally transfixed by the music coming from inside a small temple, which I later realized was the ancient Naina Devi (Goddess) temple. I couldn't move. I stopped dead in my tracks. It was one of the most powerful feelings I've ever had. Finally, I inched closer to be able to hear better when someone who was going in saw me and took me in with him. The music was so intense, so powerful. I'd certainly never heard anything like this in any of the temples in Long Island where I grew up! It was alive and real. Later I realized that this was the first time I heard the "Hanuman Chalisa" (prayer/ hymn to the monkey god Hanuman), which was to become one of the main chants I sing. Every single light in my being went on. I knew that *this* was it, and I had to get more. From that moment on, I became a kirtan hound. Whenever I heard that there was chanting, I went to listen.

One night I heard chanting coming from behind the hotel where I was staying. It turned out that a family of *dhobis* (washermen) lived there and would sing what I later found out was *qawali* (sacred Sufi vocal music), sung once a week on the Muslim holy day. The only way to hear them was through the grate near the ceiling in my bathroom, so I'd stand on an overturned bucket that we used to take our bath in and press my face against the grill. All of these chants were calling me back home. Everywhere I turned, I was amazed to be finding this new way to plug in.

I felt so comfortable in India, so familiar with everything, that I tried to immerse myself completely. I wore Indian clothes, tied my hair up on top of my head like the *sadhus* (wandering holy men), and walked around barefoot whenever I could. Maharaj-ji lovingly tolerated all of this, but as time went on, it was clear that becoming a Hindu was not something he encouraged in any way. Even though we spent time with Maharaj-ji in Hindu temples, it was about love, not religion. He honored all religions as true paths to the Divine and had Muslim, Sikh, Jain, and Christian devotees as well as Hindus. In time, I'd realize that there was no sense dressing up who I am. I had to learn to look inside and find who I am, not try to act the part of what I imagined was "holy." But that would take a while.

Chanting on the roof of the temple in Brindavan, 1971. *(Courtesy of Balaram Das.)*

Go naked if you want,
Put on animal skins.
What does it matter till you see the inward Ram?

— Kabir[2]

THROUGH THE EYES OF LOVE

Before I went to India, I meditated, did yoga, and became a vegetarian. I had a lot invested in being a "spiritual" person. When I got to Maharaj-ji, however, all of these things that I'd been doing to "help myself" began to fall away naturally. That's how it was being with him. In the intensity of the love, everything that was in the way—even so-called spiritual practices, especially if done with the heavy feeling of *I'm doing this because it's good for me*—would simply fall away. That feeling was a wall that separated me from the sweet, powerful intimacy of his love. I couldn't stand anything to be in between him and me. Especially me.

> *Burning with longing-fire,*
> *wanting to sleep with my head on your doorsill,*
> *my living is composed only of this trying*
> *to be in your presence.*

> — Rumi[3]

The feeling that I had while sitting with Maharaj-ji was indescribable. I was gazing at all of the beauty in the world. Can you imagine all of the beauty in the world condensed and shining brilliantly in one person? When we fall in love with someone, that's what we're seeing: all of the love in our own being is projected onto the screen of the loved one. Maharaj-ji merged with Infinite Love, so when his other devotees and I looked at him, we were looking directly into the light coming from the projector, rather than what was being shown on the screen. Then there was the feeling of being at home, so totally at home. My heart was at ease with itself. I was right where I wanted to be. *Incredible!*

Maharaj-ji showed me over and over that he knew exactly what I was going through and that he was right there with me all the time. He knew everything about me. He knew what I'd done in the morning, from what I ate for breakfast to what I was feeling when I walked across the bridge to the temple. He knew about my life before I even met him. He showed me in so many little ways that he had always been with me and was with me every moment.

One day I was sitting near him at teatime and saw the cook bringing out the bucket of clay cups and the teapot. The cook started to pour cups of tea and hand them to people. I thought, *I'll help him serve the tea.* Then I thought, *No, no, no, I don't want to do that. That's just my ego. I don't want to be willful. I want to be in the flow.* Then I thought, *Yes, I will serve tea. No, it's just ego, I'm not going to do that. Yes, I'll serve the tea. Yes. No.*

Maharaj-ji suddenly looked down at me with a look of bemused impatience and said, "Would you just serve the tea?"

It was my great good karma to sit around in that space with this being who knew *everything* . . . and still loved us. His love was not based on what we did or what we didn't do or what we thought or what we didn't think. His love was based on reality, the way things actually are. It was based on our *Being,* not on who or what *we* thought we were. His love was (and is) a powerful force that constantly drew us into ourselves, and awakened us over and over from our dreamlike lives.

One late afternoon the devotees were sitting around Maharaj-ji. It was quiet, the sun was setting, birds were singing, and we were enjoying the beauty of the evening. I'd just noted to myself how peaceful this all was when he turned to me and said, "Watch this." He asked a simple question in a very soft voice, like, "Is the weather warm in America?" All at once, the group erupted. Somebody said, "It depends on where you are." Another started talking about the various regions, and another about the seasons. People started arguing with each other—it was chaos! Then he casually looked over at me with a mischievous smile, as if to say, *See, you thought it was peaceful. But this is what it's really like just under the surface.*

Maharaj-ji played with us to draw us out of our shells and into the love, because it is the power of that loving that makes it possible to overcome the feeling of being separate and alone. Every time I got lost in my thoughts, all I had to do was come back, and there he was.

ा॒॔ म ८/ऩ॒ ट ़न॑गॅ ७॔॑ट ८/ऩ ॔॔॑/ऩ

After some time, more Westerners arrived. The "Journey to the East" was a popular adventure in those days, and the Westerners who found their way to Maharaj-ji came from all parts of America and various European countries. People came and went according to their individual desires and visa requirements. In the early days, there were maybe 20 or 25 of us staying at the hotel in Nainital at any given time (later, in other settings, the group of Westerners almost doubled). We'd arrive at the temple alone or in small groups. There was no set "program," no schedule we adhered to, but most of us did go to the temple almost every day. We'd often be handed this little yellow booklet with a picture of a flying monkey on it. I had about 50 of them in my room, but they were written in Hindi.

One day I finally asked somebody, "What *is* this booklet?" I was told that it was a prayer to Hanuman. We knew that people considered Maharaj-ji to be an incarnation or manifestation of

Hanuman, so I thought, *Cool! Maybe if we learn this prayer, we could sing it to him. We could kind of bribe him to spend more time with us.* So that was our reason for learning all 40 verses of the "Hanuman Chalisa"—anything to spend more time with Maharaj-ji!

Here's an image of the *original* Hanuman Chalisa booklet.

It worked! That's how we started singing. Otherwise, he'd just send us to the back of the temple and let us stew in our stuff until he called us. *What's he doing with us? Why are we back here? What am I doing here? How long can I stand this? There's nothing happening.* Then some devotee would come and say, "Come quick, Maharaj-ji's calling." We'd run to Maharaj-ji and he'd say, "Sing. *Kirtan karo.*" So we'd sing, and then he'd send us away again.

All I wanted was to be with him. Maharaj-ji made me so crazy with love that the one overriding feeling I had while I was with him was the desire, the need, to be as close to him as possible. I tried everything from jumping over walls to bribing drivers of the Indian devotees to tell us where he'd gone. When I wasn't with him, I burned with longing. I didn't care about chanting or meditating or doing any so-called spiritual practices. But he knew what was coming.

He was always running away from us or sending us away. Maharaj-ji used to say, "My mantra is *'Jao!'*" (This is the Hindi term for "Go away!") We asked him why he sent us away and he replied, "Attachment grows both ways." One of Lord Krishna's other names is *Mohan,* which means, "He who causes the whole universe to become attached to him." Maharaj-ji drew us in and allowed us to become attached to him. He knew how much we could withstand before getting unbalanced and "losing it." Then he would send us away, or run away, like Krishna did, and like the Gopis of Brindavan (the town on the plains where Krishna spent his boyhood), we'd be left desolate and longing for him. It was his way of purifying our hearts through the fire of love.

After traveling by buses and trains for days to see him, people would get there and bow down to him, and he'd say, "Good, you've come! Now go. Everything will be all right."

Maharaj-ji was once talking to a devotee who used to go to the ashram of another guru. He was curious about what it would be like at Kainchi, so he'd come to visit. Maharaj-ji was praising the chanting and prayers and many kinds of spiritual practices that were done at that guru's ashram. He said, "That's very good. Here it is just *aao* [come], *khao* [eat], *jao* [go]."

There was a woman in the group of Westerners from Chicago who'd been a taxi driver. Maharaj-ji also knew that I'd driven a school bus. One day, he said to both of us, "You see that car over there?" pointing at a car across the road from the temple. We said, "Yeah." He said, "Go look at it."

So the two of us walked over and stood there. I said, "You lookin' at it?" And she said, "Yeah, I'm lookin' at it."

We went back, and he asked, "Good car?"

"Sure, looks like a good car."

"Okay." He kept talking to us for another five minutes or so, then he got up and walked across the courtyard. Instead of going into his little room, which we called his "office," he walked out of the temple and over the bridge, got into the car, and the driver drove him away. We had no idea how long he'd be gone. It could have been for *months!* We literally never knew when he'd disappear. Thankfully, that particular time he came back later that day.

I lived in the temple through the summer rainy season and the fall of 1972. That year Maharaj-ji stayed in Kainchi until late

October. One morning we saw that some of the temple workers were being sent home. I began to panic. *What if he sent me away? What would I do? How could I get through a day without seeing him?* I went and hid in the back of the temple. I was sitting there, anxiously wondering what was going to happen, when I heard footsteps coming down the walkway toward where I was hiding. It was one of my guru-brothers. Maharaj-ji had called him over and said, "Go get Krishna Das. He's hiding in the back of the temple. Bring him here."

I walked to where he was sitting as if I were on the way to my own execution. I bowed to Maharaj-ji and, when I looked up, he whispered, "Quick! Pack your bags and catch the next train to Brindavan. I'll meet you there tomorrow. Don't tell anyone." *Yahooo!* So my guru-brother and I ran to our rooms and got our stuff all packed. We were walking across the bridge, carrying all of our luggage—trunks of books, musical instruments, and a huge duffel bag of clothes and blankets—when we met the other two guru-brothers who were living in the temple at that time. They asked, "What's going on?"

"Nothing." We just kept walking. Of course, they also made it to Brindavan the day after we did.

But we couldn't hold Maharaj-ji. There was no way to buy his attention, and we couldn't get him to look at us. We couldn't *give* him anything; he didn't want anything. We tried to give him money—some of the Westerners had money and they wanted to make a donation to the temple—but he wouldn't take it. He said, "All of the money in the universe is mine, even the money in America."

Maharaj-ji was completely free. It was only God, everywhere, all the time. One time Maharaj-ji was in the village of Brindavan in the middle of the summer. It was very hot. He was walking down the street, and coming toward him in the other direction was a *baba*—a sadhu or yogi with long, matted hair. They had known

34

each other many years before in the mountains. They hugged and were so happy to see each other.

This other baba said to Maharaj-ji, "Oh, now I've found you again after all these years! We'll stay together and it will be great."

But Maharaj-ji said, "No, no, no, brother, you don't want to stay with me. I'm constantly surrounded by worldly people, householders, nothing but problems and stuff. You're a sadhu, a saint; you don't want to be around me."

The sadhu said, "Oh, please take me with you! I want to be with you again; it's been so long!"

Maharaj-ji tried to dissuade him, "No, no, you don't want to be with me. I'm with worldly people all the time."

"Oh Baba, please!"

Maharaj-ji said, "Okay, okay, *chalo* [let's go]. I'm on my way to Mathura." In the middle of the day, in the summer heat, they started walking together to Mathura, which was about 15 miles away. In those days there was a 10- or 12-mile stretch with nothing but desert. No villages, no nothing. They kept walking, walking, and walking, and their thirst was growing intense. Finally, in the distance, they saw a well and ran to it. Maharaj-ji got there first.

There was a woman drawing water with a bucket. Maharaj-ji put his hands out and said, "Ma! Give me something to drink!" She poured the water in his hands, and he began to drink. As he was drinking, the other baba arrived. He had a *kamandalu,* a gourd pot, with him. It was his only possession. He put his pot out for the woman, who poured water into it, and he began to drink. While he was drinking, Maharaj-ji started chatting with the woman. He asked, "Where are you from? What village? What's your name? What's your caste?" It turned out that she was an untouchable.

When the sadhu heard this, he flipped out. In the caste system, untouchables are in fact *untouchable.* People from other castes, especially *Brahmins* (who are of the highest caste), are not supposed to come into contact with them. This baba was a Brahmin, which Maharaj-ji also was. But Maharaj-ji wasn't bound by any system; he treated all people the same. The baba started screaming at Maharaj-ji, "What have you done!" He threw his pot down on the ground and broke it. "You are responsible for this. Look what's happened! Look what you got me into! I needed this pot. It was my only possession, and now it's ruined and impure! I can't use it anymore!"

Maharaj-ji pretended that he didn't understand and said, "What? What? *Kya baat?* What's the matter? What happened? Oh," he said, "I thought you were a sadhu! Oh, I'm so sorry, I thought you were a saint! What is all this attachment? What is all this anger? What is this? Where did this come from?"

Hearing these words and realizing his attachment, the baba fell down at Maharaj-ji's feet and, as Maharaj-ji later related, "He washed my feet with his tears and went back to the mountains to finish his *sadhana,* or spiritual work." Maharaj-ji had warned him, "Don't hang out with me! Anything could happen." And it had. Anyone who was attracted to Maharaj-ji, who was beyond all attachment, was consciously or unconsciously offering their hearts for purification.

We want to be near these great beings because of the love, but anything inside us that can burn will start burning. Everything that is hidden is going to show. Being around him, I became more aware of the stuff that took me out of the love; my thoughts, desires, and emotions, which were running totally out of control, came between us. Drawn by the power of his love, like moths to a flame, the other devotees and I were purified by that fire. There was nowhere to get *away* from it. And we didn't *want* to get away. We wanted to *be* in that love, but in order to *be* in that love, our stuff had to burn away. The process still continues in a different way.

There's a Rumi poem that goes:

> *I would love to kiss you.*
> *The price of kissing is your life.*
>
> *Now my loving is running toward my life shouting,*
> *What a bargain, let's buy it.*

— Rumi[4]

When Maharaj-ji looked at me or talked to me, I would feel as if I were flowing into him like a river flows into the ocean. When he turned away for a minute or didn't throw me a piece of fruit for a day or two, I could not keep it together. People would bring fruit as an offering for Maharaj-ji, and the minute it touched the takhat he was lying on, he'd start tossing pieces in all directions. If fruit was flying but none came my way, depression, anger, or any one of a million emotions would explode as I became distracted by the thought that I was too impure to get a piece of fruit from Maharaj-ji. If people around me were carrying away armloads of bananas and apples and I got nothing, I'd lose my connection to the love. Then when I thought that killing myself was the only reasonable thing to do, I might turn my head for a second to see something, and suddenly I'd get hit right in the heart by a banana. When I'd look up, he'd be smiling right at me. He knew exactly what was going on. No matter how many times I closed down, he'd reach in and open me up.

He didn't teach with words. He'd shine on me like the sun, and I'd bloom. When the clouds came in between us, I saw that they were my own clouds. Then I would sit there freaking out, *What the fuck! I can't do anything about this.* Then he'd throw me a banana and giggle. Even if my eyes were closed, he'd hit me with an apple right in the heart. Just like that, every time. He was completely aware of what was going on in my head and my heart and my life. And he was a master of the dance. He was dancing while the other devotees and I were tripping over ourselves on the floor. The minute I'd fall down, he'd pick me up. He'd put me right, and then I'd trip up again and he'd pick me up again.

When Maharaj-ji would throw a piece of fruit at one of us or even simply say our names, it made us feel good, feel loved. Unfortunately, I could only retain that feeling of love for a certain amount of time before my natural tendency to crash would reassert itself. But he'd do it again and again with everyone, and every time he'd look at us in a special way. We got very attached to him. It was like being attached to your partner in a relationship, especially at the beginning when it's only *that* partner looking at you in *that* way that makes you feel such love. But because I never felt judged by him, I always wanted to come back to the love.

In a relationship with another person, you can buy flowers, send candy, go to a movie, eat dinner by candlelight, and so forth, keeping your partner turned toward you in the process. It was not like that with Maharaj-ji. There was nothing I could *do* to get him to pay attention to me. There's a phrase in the classic Indian tale of the *Ramayana* (the story of Lord Ram) that Maharaj-ji used to repeat: "Ram loves only love," which means that love only responds to love. There can be no manipulation in love. You can't rip a heart open, or force a heart to feel love. When we know that, then we know the truth, and when we open to that love, we allow it to flow.

So when I couldn't get his attention, how did I sustain the love? I *didn't!* I wanted to commit suicide. Twenty times a day. I wanted it so bad, but my capacity to stay in that feeling was so limited. If it didn't feel like it was coming to me at that moment, I'd start to panic and crumble. I also understood that this was my own stuff, because *he* never turned off. He was always right there, right here! And the minute I dropped my stuff, we would be *here* in love together. *Every single time.*

There is a great story about the Ba'al Shem Tov, the founder of Hasidism. (*Ba'al Shem Tov* means "Master of the Good Name.") He had been hiding his spiritual light, but the time had come for him to reveal himself in the world. Another rabbi, Rav Naftali, was traveling home from a wedding and stopped at the inn that was run by the Ba'al Shem Tov and his wife. The Ba'al Shem Tov took his horses and gave the rabbi a strange smile. He asked if the rabbi would be staying with them for the Sabbath. The rabbi got upset because the Sabbath was four days away and, of course, he would not be staying in such a rustic, out-of-the-way place for so many days.

Every day, this rabbi would leave the inn on his way home, only to get very confused and suddenly find himself back again at the inn. On the day before the Sabbath, he left again, determined to get home, but on this day he had a total meltdown. He saw that all beings suffer terribly and had no way of freeing themselves from their pain. He saw that an abyss surrounded all beings and none could cross over to touch or be touched by another being. Everyone was completely isolated in their agony. The rabbi's heart was crushed, and he began to get angry at God. Then he had a vision. A man appeared in the midst of all this suffering and filled all space with love. All of the beings in the world clung to him and, seeing themselves though the eyes of his love, were joined and found comfort in the world. When he opened his eyes, Rabbi Naftali was back at the inn and realized that the man smiling at him and holding the reins of his horses was the man in his vision, the Ba'al Shem Tov.

This is how a real guru works. We see ourselves and each other through his eyes, the eyes of total love, and in that love we are freed from our darkness, grief, and isolation.

That was the way Maharaj-ji looked at us.

A typical darshan in the back of the Kainchi temple, 1971. I am standing in front of Maharaji with hands joined. *(Courtesy of Chaitanya.)*

THE MEDICINE OF THE NAME

𝓣𝓫 𝓵𝓲𝓻

Maharaj-ji was always pushing our buttons and stretching our emotions, bringing everything to the surface and then dissolving it in love. Even so, there was never any feeling of being manipulated, no power tripping. Everything he did was out of love and compassion and designed to help us be free of the things that caused us pain. I was sitting there looking at all of the love in the universe: the light, the beauty, the love, the sweetness . . . everything was right there. He was so irresistible. All of the beauty of the universe was wrapped up in that blanket.

In those days, I naturally thought that he was outside of me. I didn't understand that he was in the process of changing that. It would take a long time. I had to develop the ability to keep myself turned in the direction of that light. I read the books that said the guru was not outside—*still,* to me it looked as if he was outside of me. When I was grabbing on to his foot for dear life, it seemed like his foot, not my foot.

He never thought that. With human beings, it's as if we're loving from the outside in, but Maharaj-ji was loving us from the inside out. He had merged with the One, the very core of our being, and was radiating outward, transforming our thoughts, emotions, and the way we saw ourselves.

I have lived on the lip
of insanity, wanting to know reasons,
knocking on a door. It opens.
I've been knocking from the inside!

— Rumi[5]

We think we are who we *think* we are. That's what is called *maya*, illusion. The true guru knows the truth and is not affected by maya. He has become the whole universe; to him, there is nothing outside of the true Self, the One, but he still appears like a normal human being, at least most of the time. Extraordinary!

The *sadguru*, the true guru, is not outside of us. That light might be temporarily located in the body of a physical being, but the guru is not the body. A true guru is one with the universe and everything in it. We are also not the body, but we identify with it. When we have a relationship with a true guru, we're relating to him as we see him to be, but he is relating to us as who we are in reality.

As Albert Einstein once noted:

> A human being is a part of the whole, called by us the "universe," a part limited in time and space. He experiences himself, his thoughts and feelings, as something separated from the rest—a kind of optical delusion of his consciousness. This delusion is a kind of prison for us, restricting us to our personal desires and to affection for a few persons nearest to us. Our task must be to free ourselves from this prison by widening our circle of compassion to embrace all living creatures and the whole of nature in its beauty.

We see ourselves as separate and different from other people. On the level of thoughts, physicality, and emotions, we certainly seem to be. This is the "optical delusion," and yet it is what we experience. My stuff revolves around a different planet than yours. You have your planet, I have mine. But on the deepest level, our planets are actually each a reflection of the same thing—the Self, the One—like the moon reflected in different pools: one moon, same light, many reflections. When the pool of water is calm and there is no debris floating on the surface, all of the reflections are identical. To the extent that we experience that, the way we live our lives changes. The true guru gradually frees us from this "optical delusion," whether he's guiding us from "within" as a manifestation of our own true Self, or from another human body that appears to be "outside" of us. Whether or not we meet the guru outside of us at some point in time, all of us have the guru inside as that place within us that *knows*.

Getting to the place inside that *knows* we are One requires practice. My main formal practice is chanting the Names of God. The practice of the repetition of the Name invokes a space or a place inside of us, a presence that's always here. It isn't subject to the vagaries of our thoughts and emotions—the ups and downs, the ins and outs. Chanting the Divine Names invokes the inner heart, which is the presence that lives within us.

This heart is not an emotional state; emotions come and go. It is also not referring to the physical pump that resides in the chest. The heart is an abode, our home, the place in each of us where we know who we actually are. This abode is deeper than thoughts and deeper than emotions. And that presence, of course, is our own presence: who we actually are underneath who and what we think we are, underneath the inner dialogue that's always going on about everything. This "heart" is called *chidakasha.* It's the sky of the mind, of consciousness, our true Being, not located at any one place. Embracing and encompassing everything, nothing is outside of it. It is home.

> *The heart means the very core of one's being,*
> *without which there is nothing whatever.*
>
> — Ramana Maharshi[6]

These Names that we sing, on the deepest level, are the names of who we truly are. The names of what's in there—not what we *think* is in there, which is our story line, but what's really in there. That place is pure love, pure truth, pure enjoyment. *Pure,* meaning "as it is." We don't make it. It exists naturally as it is inside of us. But because it's underneath everything, we're always looking for it. Having been born into Western culture, we're programmed to look outside for everything, so we look for that feeling in other people and in "stuff." Of course, we have difficulty finding it in a real, lasting way. Until we can connect to that place inside of ourselves, we can't really find it in another person.

Being born in the West is a mixed blessing. On the one hand, it's wonderful to live where our basic needs of life are fairly easily acquired. On the other hand, we pay a high internal price for our material comfort.

We were born with Mickey Mouse, Donald Duck, and television. We weren't born into a culture that recognizes there is a spiritual path. The fact that we even know the path exists is extraordinary. We were raised in a culture that is totally outward, or materially directed, and taught that happiness comes from "things." So we spend our lives pressing the buttons we think will bring us the feelings we long for: the car button, the clothes button, the jewelry and new-hairdo buttons, the relationship button, the money button, and so on. We spend our time trying to get stuff and hold on to stuff, using stuff to get more stuff. When we don't have stuff, we worry about getting it. When we have stuff, we worry about losing it. It's a no-win situation. So it's often difficult to turn our focus inward, to something that's totally invisible and for the most part unrecognized and unacknowledged in our Western culture.

It's as if we're living on the front lawn of our own home. We've been locked out of ourselves for so long that we forget there is a house to live in. We buy all kinds of stuff and put it on the lawn. Yes, all that furniture and that expensive flat-screen HDTV are on the lawn. Then when they get rained on and ruined, causing us unhappiness, we think that that's the way it has to be. We've forgotten what a house is for. We've forgotten that there even *is* a house. We've forgotten that there is shelter inside of our own hearts.

The guru calls us up from the phone inside the house, "Hey! Look in the window! I'm inside here. Come on in!" We know all the right words—"God is within," "Guru, God, and Self are one"—but we're talking from outside of ourselves, sitting on the front lawn. That's why we Westerners can do so much practice without it actually changing our lives. It's relatively easy to *do* practice; we're great at doing stuff, but we're even better at making sure that it doesn't have any real effect on us. Why? Because we've lost that connection to our simple inner being. We don't trust ourselves, and we don't know how to be good to ourselves.

Once I was hanging out with a baba who was *mauna,* silent. He hadn't spoken in 12 years. He would communicate by writing with his finger on the palm of his hand. He was talking about how great India was. I asked, "So why did we get born in America?"

He wrote, letter by letter, "F-a-s-t-e-r."

The West is a good place to do sadhana, spiritual practice, because most of us have our basic requirements met. Most of us have places to live and enough to eat. It's not that way with the majority of the people in this world, who don't have the time or opportunity to practice a path in the ways we can. People are looking for food. They're dodging bombs or running away from invading armies.

Think of how many different lives you can live during one single lifetime in the West. You want to be a doctor, go to school. You want to be a cabbie, get a driver's license. You want to be a musician, play. Similarly, if you want to find your way inside, you can do spiritual practice.

Over time, the practice of chanting has changed the way I feel about the world around me because it is changing the way I feel about myself. Chanting uncovers the happiness, beauty, and love *inside* of us. It shows us that we *have* that already. That's a big thing. My mother didn't know. My father didn't know. Nobody in my family knew, so I never learned. But I had this crazy longing inside of me to connect with something that seemed to be missing. That's why I went to India. Something inside told me, *They know it over there. You'll find it there.* And I found my guru there, who led me to the practice of chanting the Name.

Chanting is not really about music at all. Maharaj-ji gave me the medicine. When a child has to take medicine, it has to be hidden in a sweet syrup. In the same way, the medicine of the Name is hidden in the sweet syrup of the music. The result of the medicine working is the happiness we get from the removal of our illness. In the case of chanting, the medicine of the Name removes the illness of looking outside for love, and awakens an inner strength and confidence and a feeling of well-being as we move deeper into our own hearts.

R.D. Ranade quotes the great saint Tukaram in *Mysticism in Maharashtra:*

> "By the power of the Name of God, one shall come to know what one does not know. One shall see what cannot be seen. One will be able to speak what cannot be spoken. One shall meet what cannot be ordinarily met. Incalculable will be the gain of uttering the Name," says Tuka.

The challenge is to keep taking my medicine.

The more I sing, and the deeper I go, the more *real* the presence of love becomes inside of me and the less it has to do with anything Indian or Western or Tibetan or anything external. It has to do with Being. To me, these Names represent the presence of love at the deepest level in my own heart. When I sing, what I want to do is enter into that presence as deeply and with as much intensity and concentration as I can. For me, my guru is the essence of that love, the door into that love, but even so, I can't say that I'm thinking of him as he was when I knew him in the body. Bringing him to mind helps me find that place, and then there's no thinking about anything.

The mind should be kept in the heart as long
as it has not reached the Highest End.
This is wisdom, and this is liberation.
Everything else is only words.

— Maitri Upanishad, 6.24

Ram Ram, in Maharaj-ji's handwriting.

THE HEART OF PRACTICE:
JUST DO IT

$\overleftarrow{\text{ᏚᏅᏐᏆ}}$

One of the first times I was ever interviewed was by a writer from *Yoga Journal,* who asked me to talk about chanting as a spiritual practice. I was taken by surprise. The truth is that I'd never thought of it like that before. Of course, that's what chanting is, but I didn't have it in my mind that I was doing a "practice." I was just trying to get my life together, so I didn't have much to tell him. Then he asked, "Well, how do you sing?" I thought about it and remembered when I'd gotten my junior driving permit. I was driving in my car alone for the first time and going to my girlfriend's house. I turned on the radio and *our* song came on. The way I sang that song at that moment is the way I chant.

I was living in the temple with Maharaj-ji in the fall of 1972, during the festival known as Durga puja, a fire ceremony that goes on for nine days and celebrates the destruction of various demons by the goddess who manifests after being prayed to by all of the gods. It is one of the biggest festivals of the year, and many of the devotees would come to the temple to stay with Maharaj-ji for the entire period. Because of the nature of Indian culture, it was also one of the few times that his female devotees—the *Mas,* or mothers, as they're called—were able to come and be with him for an extended period. They'd all live together in the back of the temple, and at night they'd gather to sing holy songs and chant in one of the inner rooms that was off-limits to men.

I would sit outside the window of that room for hours, totally immersed in the intensity, passion, and joy that these ladies sang with. The chanting would be going on for while, and then all of a sudden there would be a scream of ecstasy as one of women went into a state of absorption in God. The sweetest thing was that when they discovered I was sitting outside and listening for so many hours, they cracked the window so that I could hear better, knowing I'd respect their privacy. This was one of my most important and life-changing experiences. I bathed myself in their devotion and opened up new rivers of love in my heart.

The heart of this practice is simply repeating the Name over and over again. Everything comes from that because it is said that everything is contained within the Name. When I can do this wholeheartedly, then I'll see if there is anything else I have to do. In the meantime, it's enough. When I'm really chanting—singing the Name and coming back to it again and again—no matter what is going on in my head, I have to let go of it. There's no option. The only option is to sing. And that's what the instruction is: *Sing*. Not to think or imagine anything; not to try to make anything happen; not to ruminate about stuff that happened earlier or might happen later . . . I just have to sing. I try to gather all of my strength together and sing, no matter what.

When I started, even if I got myself to sit down and sing, my mind was somewhere else in a second. But that's the beauty of this practice. We start from where we are. We get lost in thought, and we come back. As soon as we realize that we're gone, we come back. It's amazing. Most of us will have to do it 40 billion times a minute, but that's okay. As soon as we realize we're gone, we're already back. Then by the time we realize that, we're gone again. Thinking *I'm back* is not the same as being back. Recognizing that we're lost in thought is the first step in turning within. We can't hold on to the awareness in the same way that we clutch a cookie in our hand. It's not something we can understand or think about in our head. That's why we're asked to simply chant. The chanting begins to draw us into a deeper space in our own being, so we sit more at ease in ourselves.

Chanting is called a practice for one reason: it only works if we do it. Chanting has been my main practice for years, but it took me a long time to realize that it's only by doing it regularly that we begin to experience ourselves changing. If we want to get wet, we have to jump in the water. If we want to *stay* wet, we have to learn to swim, or at least float! We can read about sugar, people can tell us about sugar and describe the sweetness to us, but if we want to know what it tastes like, we've got to put some in our mouths. That's why we do practice: we must have our own experience. In order for it to help when difficult things in life happen—we lose someone, we get sick, we have a car accident, or someone dies— we have to do it. Over time, we'll see that we're getting stronger, making it easier to deal with difficult situations.

During the rainy season in Kainchi, Maharaj-ji used to have a bunch of guys come up from Brindavan to sing kirtan. These *kirtan walas,* as they're called, would sing *Hare Krishna* from about four in the morning until eleven at night. They'd sing in shifts, switching off to rest and eat, but it was still about six hours of chanting a day for each of them. One year, toward the end of the season, just before the ashram was to be closed for the winter, one of these guys tried to seduce one of the Western women. This was a big no-no. Maharaj-ji found out about it, and in about ten minutes all of the kirtan walas were loaded onto the back of a truck with their stuff and taken to the train to go back to Brindavan.

One of the Indians in the temple asked Maharaj-ji, "Who's going to sing now? You just kicked out the kirtan walas." Maharaj-ji said, "The Westerners." Actually, this wasn't good news to me. The little room where the kirtan was sung was around the corner from where Maharaj-ji came out and sat. So if he came out during my shift, I wouldn't be able to see him. Days could pass and I wouldn't have a chance to sit with him. Disaster!

We had one instruction: Sing. There was nothing about stopping. I'd be singing *Hare Krishna* with a couple of other devotees, bored out of my mind: *Hare Krishna Hare Krishna Krishna Krishna Hare Hare.* . . . We couldn't stop, we had to keep going—that was the instruction. It was torture. My whole life passed before my eyes when I was singing. I remembered everything from when I was a kid. I relived my life about a thousand times up to that moment. Even though I was trying to pay some attention to what I was doing, I was not very successful. I'd be singing *Hare Krishna Hare Krishna,* then I'd remember my ex-girlfriend back in the States. All of a sudden *Hare Krishna* would get a bit juicier. I'd sing like that for a while. Then I'd remember that she broke up with me, and I'd start experiencing rage and anger and hurt—all the while, the mantra kept going on.

Even though I didn't realize it at the time, I was lucky. There was nowhere to go. I mean, how many times can you get up and go to the bathroom? I was supposed to be singing, so I just kept singing . . . and, because there was no option, nowhere to go, no channel to change, some part of me finally gave up. I began to relax into the chanting. And then quite unexpectedly, I had my first experience of the power of chanting. I noticed that my thoughts didn't stick to me the way they usually did and that I wasn't completely lost in them. I'd see the thoughts come, and while I might "be thinking" for a while, then I'd see the thoughts go. All of a sudden there were holes in the endless flow of completely unconscious thinking. And those holes were filled with *Hare Krishna.*

Thoughts would come and go but wouldn't take me with them. I wasn't making any effort to *avoid* thoughts, but the continued repetition of the Name had naturally gotten sweeter and I was enjoying being in it. It was as if I now had more room in me and the thoughts would float by like clouds, coming and going across the sky. No one was more surprised than I was.

I'm reminded of these words by Swami Sivananda:

> The name of God, chanted correctly or incorrectly, knowingly or unknowingly, carefully or carelessly, is sure to give the desired result. The glory of the name cannot be established through reasoning and intellect. It can certainly be experienced or realised only through devotion, faith and constant repetition of the name. Every name is filled with countless potencies or *saktis* [powers].[7]

One day I headed for the bathroom while the other devotees kept singing. I usually tried to sneak a quick moment with Maharaj-ji, but he'd inevitably motion for me not to come. On this day I didn't even try to go sit with him and went straight to the bathroom. On my way back, though, without thinking about it, I went and sat down with him. He didn't stop me, as if it were the most natural thing for me to do. He was talking to a couple of other devotees, and I was sitting there gazing at him. The sound of the kirtan was coming over the loudspeaker, and I remember thinking how beautiful it was. The next thing I knew, Maharaj-ji was patting me on the head, saying, "Very good. Very good. Go sing." I'd disappeared into the sound of the chant and hadn't even realized it!

Maharaj-ji planted the seeds of this practice in me. It wasn't until many years after he died that I was able to pick up the thread of what he'd given me at that time. I had to be forced to give the practice time to work on me, to let me experience what happened when my inner direction changed. Instead of constantly looking out there—*take this, take that, buy this, look at this, go there, eat this*—I experienced how the chanting started to move me *inward*, into myself.

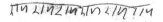

If we aren't doing a practice, we don't realize how "gone" we are most of the time. We float through our dream day, totally unaware, running on automatic, reacting and being pushed around by our thoughts and emotions. When we begin to do a practice, we begin to see how we waste our time.

Even though our thoughts take us away—and many different memories, fantasies, and impressions continually arise—we can always return again to the repetition of the Name. Every single time we return to the practice, we are overcoming ancient innate tendencies of the mind to flow outward. Every time we come back, we are reminding ourselves where to look, and it gets deeper each time. This is why it's said that what matters isn't how many times we go away, but how many times we come back, because each time we come back, we are coming back to the singularity of the Name.

> Now it is but natural that a thing impressed consciously a hundred times is far more effective than the unconscious single impressions of a hundred different things. By simple calculation, the repeated impressions survive, and the others fade out. No single Name inhaled or exhaled is wasted, and each one progressively identifies the devotee with God.[8]

Through practice, a part of us learns what it feels like to let go of whatever takes us away, and we come back—let go, come back, let go, come back. With the constant repetition of that process, we intuitively develop the ability to let go. As time goes on and difficult experiences arise, all that work of letting go kicks in and we find ourselves more present and better able to deal with them. We are able to let go of the destructive habits and thoughts that make dealing with crises so overwhelming for us. It's the same process.

When we come into the presence of love, we can't let go fast enough. It's everything we want. That's when we experience how stuck we are. We have to practice letting go in little bits—a little bit every day—so that when those moments occur, more of who we are can get through the door. We can't get through the door carrying all of our luggage. We learn not to pack that bag with so much stuff all the time. When we're more available for those moments, they last longer. We spend less time in heavier, darker states of mind.

The Names we chant move us into a space that's a little less obsessive, a little less constricted, more open and relaxed. The idea being that once we see what's in that room, we'll *want* to go in because it feels like home.

I approach chanting in a very pragmatic way: I try not to create any fantasies in my head about what is supposed to be happening. I get to this place of simply being inside of myself. Anything that raises anticipation or creates an expectation of what is going to happen is a hindrance. To me it is not about trying to achieve ecstatic states. It is about love. I want to be there all the time. Ecstasy comes and goes. I want to get to the place where there's only *Sitaram*. I don't want to be thinking about love, I want to *be* in love and eventually *become* love.

In the words of St. Teresa of Avila:

> Remember: if you want to make progress on the path and ascend to places you have longed for, the important thing is not to think much but to love much, and so to do whatever best awakens you to love.[9]

One of the biggest obstacles to practice is the type of expectation we bring to it. For instance, if I'm leading a workshop and say, "Okay, now we're going to meditate," everybody starts to sit up straight and get tense, filled by the idea that *I am going to do something.* We expect the sky to open and nectar to pour all over us. In reality, it's not like that. We have so many expectations that when we sit down to meditate or chant, we're crippled by anxiety, evaluating what we're doing. *How's this? Is this good? Yeah, that's good. I'm watching my breath, I'm watching my breath . . . that's very good. Yeah, in, out, okay, good, okay . . .* and the ego gets a subtle stroking and feels good about itself for doing this. Practices take time. They work slowly, from the inside out. "Sudden" enlightenment takes millions and millions of births.

But if I say, "Let's sing," we just sing. We don't think about it, which short-circuits a lot of those habits of thought.

There are many ways to meditate, and all of the different ways are fine. Chanting is also meditation. We sing, make music, make noise, and let go; and we don't get stuck being a "meditator" because we're enjoying what we're doing. We're just repeating the Name for the joy of doing it. It's sneaky because we're not expecting it to work—we don't have the expectation of achieving something. We're just singing. We feel happy when we sing. It feels natural. And it is.

Problems arise when we sit down to try to *make* something happen. Because when it doesn't, we get pissed off with ourselves or with the teacher or the practice and our neurotic programming kicks in, telling us that we can't do it. We might not sit down again for a long time. Sharon Salzberg, the great meditation teacher, says, "The most important moment of practice is sitting down to do it." Simply sitting down to practice is such a big thing. So when I chant, I just sing. That's my job—to sing and to sing and to sing. I give it my best shot. I really try to concentrate, to pay attention, to keep coming back to the chanting. I listen to the group, then I listen to myself, I listen to the group . . . I try to stay in that back-and-forth flow of the sound of the Name going on.

That's the practice. If I feel light and happy, that's nice, but I still keep singing. I notice those thoughts and keep singing. If I feel heavy and tired, I keep singing. No matter what I feel or think, I keep singing. This is how the chanting begins to liberate us from constantly getting sucked in by our feelings. It frees us from all that. We don't push the thoughts away; we're just singing because the singing—the chanting—will take us deeper and deeper. We let go of whatever pulls us out of it and come back to the sound of the Name. And then we have our own experience of what it is. This is how we continually locate that feeling of presence within. We're not trying to have any particular experience or make anything happen; we're simply listening to the Names as they arise.

One day two old guys, dressed like sadhus, showed up at the temple and asked Maharaj-ji if they could stay there. Maharaj-ji said they could stay, but that every day they should sit in front of the Hanuman temple and sing *Sitaram*—just *Sitaram*. Pretty good rent! So the next morning they were out there singing *Sitaram* while we were hanging out waiting for Maharaj-ji to come out. They were sitting across from each other, singing back and forth. They didn't have any instruments—no bangers or clangers. The first guy would chant *Sitaram Sitaram Sitaram jai Sitaram,* and the other guy would repeat *Sitaram Sitaram Sitaram jai Sitaram.* Back and forth, back and forth. Then, I don't know, maybe he got bored, but the first guy went *Sitaram Sitaram Sitaram jai Hanuman.* And the other guy went "Whoa! Jazz!" and pretty soon they were having a party, riffing on the holy Names: *Rama Lakshman Janaki Bolo Hanumana Ki!*

All of a sudden, from his rooms in the back, Maharaj-ji's voice bellowed out like thunder through the foot-thick cement walls: *Sitaram!* And it was back to *Sitaram Sitaram Sitaram jai Sitaram.*

It was the first time I intuitively understood that awareness, paying attention, was the key to practice. We don't have to *do* anything but pay attention. This is a great relief. We are allowed to release our usual expectations or anxieties about achieving something. We have permission to lay them down and relax. All we have to do is pay attention to the chant, to *Sitaram.*

GRADUALLY BUT INEVITABLY

When I sing kirtan or do workshops, people often ask the meanings of the chants. Who is this Ram whose Name we're chanting? Who is Krishna? Who is Shiva? The reason I don't talk about the meanings of the chants is because I don't really know. When I began singing, I was singing to Maharaj-ji and for Maharaj-ji. The chanting brought me directly to that place of love, which all of these Names represent.

All of these Names have come to us through the stories of the various incarnations or manifestations that the Divine has taken in order to destroy suffering in the world. These stories can be found in the sacred writings of India, the *Puranas,* the *Bhagavatam,* the *Ramayana* of Valmiki, and the *Ramcaritmanas* of Tulsidas, as well as many others. Yet even though I've been going to India for the last 40 years, I've never made a deep study of these ancient scriptures. I'm moved by their beauty and depth, of course, but it's not the focus of my practice.

There's a practice called *bhajan,* which is singing beautiful love songs to God, very much like the singing of Christian gospel songs in that they tell the stories of the Divine Beings. They create wonderful warm feelings in our hearts and can be very helpful in creating an atmosphere of quietness and openness. But I'm a depressed guy. That stuff is hard for me to get into most of the time. I just want to get *here,* get present. I don't know anything else. What I do know is that when I chant, it feels right. I'm not trying to create any wonderful, loving story line to go with that or use a loving story line to get into it. I was never able to do that. In India, even when I don't understand the language and people are singing, the *feeling* is so strong that it draws me in. I don't have to understand the words.

The deepest meanings of all of these Names and the reality of all of the deities worshipped in all spiritual traditions is beyond the mind, beyond anything that can be understood or experienced intellectually. As Maharaj-ji said, "Whatever we experience and learn through the mind and the senses is not the truth." All of the deities have their own stories of how they manifest in the world, especially to help at times when there is great darkness and suffering. When I chant, however, I'm not thinking about that.

When I'm chanting, I'm just chanting. That's all I know. I'm moving into a quieter, more spacious moment, and sometimes I move into the presence of love. The *antarayamin,* the indwelling presence of love, attracts us through any form that appeals to us, which leads us into our own true heart. It's like water and ice: ice looks different than water, but actually it's nothing but water. Krishna, Shiva, and the other deities are like the ice, different forms of the One.

To quote Anandamayi Ma:

> When you have become attracted to and get in touch with a particular Divine form, as you become more absorbed in it you one day find out that He is indeed the formless. Then you see that He is sakara [with form] as well as nirakara [without form] as well as beyond both.[10]

In India, there's a festival called Holi, which celebrates the *raslila,* when Krishna danced under the full moon with all of the *gopis* (milkmaids who worshipped Krishna as the Beloved).

He manifested himself in a different form for each one of the milkmaids, making love to each one in the way she secretly desired in her heart of hearts. None knew what was going on with the others. Each one felt like she was alone with Krishna.

There is a whole tradition of devotional songs celebrating this beautiful relationship between God and His devotees. One time I was up in the hills at K.K.'s (the devotee who helped me get to India to meet Maharaj-ji) house during Holi, and devotees came from all around to sing these love songs throughout the night. These were not professional musicians; they were local people who worked and had families and regular lives, but who also carried on this ancient tradition. The younger guys started about ten at night. It was beautiful! What voices! I remember thinking, *It can't get any better than this.*

But as it got later and later and the singers got older and older, the beauty of the voice began to give way to the beauty of the heart. At four in the morning, the eldest of the devotees began to sing. His voice was cracked from a lifetime of smoking *bidis* (Indian leaf cigarettes), but the vibe when he sang was astounding. He could no longer sing totally in key or with any sweetness of voice, but his singing had become all *bhav,* all feeling. The young guys sucked me in with the beauty of their music, but as soon as the old guy started to sing, I went, *Aha! This is the real stuff.*

In India, they say that God is beyond any name or form, beyond the mind, neither male nor female. This is the ultimate statement of truth, but it is also said that the very same Ultimate Presence will take a form to answer the loving call of a devotee's heart. All of these divine beings are doorways into love—into the deepest place in our own heart. After all, God is love and love is God.

> *With us the name of everything*
> *is its outward appearance;*
> *with the Creator,*
> *the name of each thing is its inward reality.*

— Rumi[11]

That being said, I bow to all of the deities when I visit their temples. Even though I'm not experiencing them in their deepest reality, I *am* bowing to what they represent to me, which is a power and a love that's beyond the understanding of the mind but "feel-able" in the heart. All of these beings have different qualities. They're actually states of consciousness into which we can enter. As far as I understand, they're not physical beings, they're consciousness beings—states of consciousness that are available to us because they're a part of our own true Self. They allow us to enter into them through love.

It is said that everything is contained within the sound of the Name. By repeating the Name as wholeheartedly as we can, anything and everything we need to know will be revealed from within; anything and everything that needs to happen will happen without having to think about it or understand it intellectually. All of the Names come from the same Source. By repeating these Names, we're directly invoking the indwelling presence in our own hearts.

Shirdi Sai Baba has said that *Namasmarana,* or the constant inward repetition of the Name, is actually God remembering Himself within us. The power of the presence of God is carried in the Name:

> Beginning with simple repetition, gradually but inevitably, the Divine power which is hidden in it, is disclosed and takes on the character of a ceaseless uplifting of the heart, which persists through the distractions of the surface life.[12]

I love that phrase, "gradually but inevitably." It means that even if we're running through a train from the front to the back, in the opposite direction that the train is going, when the train reaches the station, so will we. So much of my life has been spent running in the wrong direction, only to find that I've wound up in the right place anyway.

So despite the fact that we don't know the true meaning of these Names, repeating them is still different from just saying the name Frank over and over. By repeating Frank, we remember every Frank we ever knew. Many images arise in the mind. But when we say *Ram,* what image do we get? Most likely, no concrete form appears. And that's the whole point. The real Ram is not a person we've met in our daily life. The real Ram lives in our own hearts and, by the repetition of the Name, we are tuning in to that essence within us. If it is something we can imagine or make up in our own heads, then it cannot take us beyond our own heads. In this way, the repetition of the Name can free us from our thoughts and allow us to be here in a deeper way.

Maharaj-ji said, "Ram's form left this world, Krishna's form left this world, but the Name stays. By reciting His Name, everything is achieved." Shaking his head, he reiterated, "Everything is achieved."

Someone once said to me, "You don't talk much about God," and I responded, "That's right, I don't." Then I asked her, "What is God?" She said she didn't know. I replied, "Neither do I, which is why I don't talk about it." Through the repetition of the Name, what is within will be uncovered and revealed to us directly and personally. So for me, there's no benefit to spending time fantasizing and conceptualizing about something that's impossible to know and understand in the mind. I won't find God by thinking.

Let me start where I am. I'm *here,* I know I'm here. Now, what's in here? Who is here? That's what I want to know. My belief is that what lives within me is that divine reality. All I have to do is uncover it. The path is a personal, individual quest for each of us. It is a journey of spirit, not necessarily having anything to do with organized religion. When we can live in spirit, meaning that which lives inside of us already, we will see it everywhere.

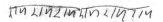

LILA

It's very difficult for people like us, who are identified with our bodies and minds, to understand the concept of *lila*—the divine play. It's called "play" because there's no selfish motive in the action. God's lila or the lila of a great saint, his or her action in the world, is done only for the sake of helping others. There is no personal motive. The saint's actions come out of the awareness of the oneness of all life and compassion for all beings. It's impossible for us to understand fully.

In a way, it's how a really good babysitter works. He or she can play games with the kids and tell them stories and get them to bed at the right time, without the children ever realizing that they're being cared for by an adult who has an agenda, which is to keep them all safe. But if there's a problem, the kids come running to the babysitter, who has the strength and wisdom to deal with it. The lilas of *avatars,* or enlightened beings, are like that. They accomplish all that they have to do for us by acting like one of us. In this way they protect us, inspire us, and set us on the right path. But when we're in danger or in need, they show us a deeper aspect of themselves, or some of their miraculous *siddhis* (powers). They are *in* the world, but not *of* it. When they manifest their divinity, *that* is lila.

On the path of devotion, one can focus on the lila of the Beloved. *Ram Lila* and *Krishna Lila* are collections of stories that tell all of the things that these divine beings did, all of the plays they enacted while they were incarnated.

िन 2/मटीम्/लि 2/म टीम

Dada was one of Maharaj-ji's great old devotees, who frequently translated for us Westerners. Although his real name was Sudhir Mukerjee, Maharaj-ji called him *Dada*, which means "elder brother" in Hindi. Once when Dada's wife called him by his real name, Maharaj-ji said, "If he is my Dada, then he is your Dada." From then on she, along with everyone else, called him Dada.

Dada used to say that when we were with Maharaj-ji we were lost in a dream, playing our parts unconsciously in his lila, but when we were away from him, we could recall the many scenes and relive and relish them to our heart's content.

Being with Maharaj-ji was like being an actor in a play, an actor who's forgotten that he's in a play. But the play was written by a realized Being—a fully awake, conscious writer—who was also pretending to be merely another actor in the play. Everything that he wrote was designed to wake us up and lead us to the same realization, freedom, and love.

One day we were sitting with Maharaj-ji in Brindavan. A number of Westerners had recently come from meditation courses. One of them was sitting up very straight with his eyes closed. Maharaj-ji looked at me and told me to ask him what he was doing. I did, and without opening his eyes, he answered, "I'm meditating."

I said, "Maharaj-ji, he says that he's meditating."

"Oh? Ask him if he wants to see real meditation."

When I asked the guy if he wanted to see real meditation, he opened his eyes and said yes.

Maharaj-ji called over one of his close devotees, Gurudatt Sharma, and told him to sit down and meditate. Gurudatt, a family man, sat down and crossed his legs and closed his eyes. Maharaj-ji told me to tell the Westerner to come over and touch Gurudatt. He gently touched him, but Maharaj-ji said, "No, no. Push him." He did, but Gurudatt was stiff and solid as a mountain. He didn't move at all. Then Maharaj-ji told this guy to cover Gurudatt's mouth and hold his nose closed, which he did. It was obvious that Gurudatt wasn't breathing. Maharaj-ji looked at the Westerner and said, "*That's* meditation."

Then he asked me and another Westerner to pick Gurudatt up and carry him to one of the nearby rooms and put him on the bed, which we did, and then we went back to sit with Maharaj-ji. After a few minutes, Maharaj-ji got up and went into the room where Gurudatt was, closing the door behind him. In about 15 minutes, the two of them came out together, arm in arm, leaning on each other like two drunkards, drunk on bliss. Maharaj-ji settled himself back down on the takhat, and Gurudatt sat below him on the ground. Maharaj-ji looked at the Westerner again and asked, "Do you understand?"

The Westerner said no. Maharaj-ji said, "You want to see it again?" Without waiting for an answer, he ordered Gurudatt to meditate again. And Gurudatt went back into meditation. Again, after a few minutes, Maharaj-ji had us carry Gurudatt into the room. I don't know about the other Westerner, but I was very affected by this demonstration and was going to find out from Gurudatt how to meditate that way myself.

The next day, Maharaj-ji gave me my chance. He asked me to drive Gurudatt to a nearby town on some business. While we were driving, I asked him if he'd practiced meditation before. I wanted to know how to do what he did. He didn't reply, so I figured that he wasn't going to answer me. After a few minutes, however, he began to speak quietly. He said, "When I first came to Maharaj-ji, he showed me so much love and affection that some of the older devotees were shocked. He was always holding my hand and caressing me and looking at me with great love. It got to the point where one day one of the devotees asked Maharaj-ji, 'What is it about this guy? How come you show him so much affection? I have been with you much longer and you don't show me that kind of love.' Maharaj-ji didn't respond, so the devotee kept badgering him.

"Finally Maharaj-ji said, 'Okay, you want to know, I'll tell you, but I am only going to say it once.' The devotee said, 'So say it.' It was only the three of us sitting in that room. Just as Maharaj-ji began to speak, someone came to the door and called this devotee. He turned his head to see who was calling him; by the time he turned back, Maharaj-ji had finished speaking. He said, 'Maharaj-ji, what did you say? I didn't hear you.' But Maharaj-ji would not repeat himself."

Gurudatt looked at me for a second and continued. "Maharaj-ji said, 'Not just this life, not just the life before, but life after life we have been together. That's why this happens.'"

We drove the rest of the way in silence.

As Namdev, the great 13th-century poet-saint, wrote, he had perfect knowledge of the Vedas (ancient Indian scriptures) and all of the schools of Indian philosophy; he had accomplished the goal of the yogis; he had himself experienced the joy of merging in the formless God; but he'd transcended all of these experiences through the grace of the saints, to find that "the secret is the Lord's Love."

Maharaj-ji's "priest" on duty at the Durga temple
in Kainchi, 1972. *(Courtesy of Chaitanya.)*

In 1972, a beautiful new temple to the Goddess Durga was
built in the temple complex at Kainchi. It was just before Durga
puja, the nine-day fall festival celebrating the Divine Mother.
Although the official opening of the temple wouldn't happen until
the spring, Maharaj-ji wanted the *murti* (consecrated statue) of the
Goddess to be seen by the devotees who came. So they brought
in a priest to sit there and do some *puja* (prayers) and give out
prasad. After a few days, they caught this priest stealing money
out of the donation box in front of the temple. He was given a few
rupees and sent home. A second priest was brought in, but in a
couple of days he was also caught stealing. He too was given a few
rupees and sent home. When a third priest was caught stealing,
the temple trust came to Maharaj-ji and said, "We're unable to
find a priest who won't steal."

Maharaj-ji pounded his chest and said, "My priest won't steal."

"Your priest? Who's your priest?"

"Krishna Das!"

I was called from the back of the temple, where I used to spend most of my time moping around in inner darkness, and was asked to sit by the temple and be the priest. I was surprised, but I took it as another way Maharaj-ji was expressing his love for me. I spent most of every day there and took care of the temple. One day I casually thought, *Since I'm sitting here, maybe I should learn some mantras.* From this beginning, all of the *Devi Puja*—the prayers and chants to the Goddess that I sing today—manifested. Maharaj-ji never said, "Learn this," yet it all happened. Lila.

One of the lilas Maharaj-ji played out with me revolved around my name. In my early days with Maharaj-ji, he called me "Driver." He'd taken the keys to Ram Dass's car away from him and given them to me. He said, "You drive." So I drove the Volkswagen bus around. He'd call "Driver!" and that was my name for what seemed like a lifetime. Everybody else was getting holy names. I was Driver. Terrific. One night I wrote in my diary: "Well, I guess that's it. I'm going to be Driver forever."

The next morning I got to the temple and was called into Maharaj-ji's room. He looked at me and said, "Arjun . . . *nay* . . . Krishna . . . *nay* . . . Krishna Das!"

I said, "*Krishna* Das?" I was a Hanuman guy. I was a Ram guy. What was with this Krishna Das stuff?

He laughed. "It's okay. Hanuman served Krishna, too."

Krishna Das means "servant of Krishna," or "servant of God." The word *Das,* meaning "servant," is from the Hanuman lineage and implies an attitude of devotional service to God. In India, there are different ways or forms of expressing love and devotion. When devotees have *dasya bhav,* this means that they see themselves as servants to God, the Master. Hanuman is the perfect servant of Ram. Other lineages emphasize different ways of relating to God: lover/Beloved, child/Parent, parent/Child, friend/the Friend.

In the Mahabharata, Krishna serves as Arjuna's charioteer in the Great War. Arjuna is the hero of the good guys, and Krishna is his friend, who also happens to be God. They survive all of these amazing battles. In those days, they used to shoot nuclear weapons with their arrows, powered by secret mantras. All through this deadly war, Arjuna's chariot survived untouched. At the end of the war, Krishna urges, "Arjuna, quickly, jump off your chariot right now." He did, and Hanuman himself leapt out of the chariot's flag—a white flag with a red monkey on it. Arjuna's chariot instantly burst into a million pieces. Krishna said, "Didn't you notice that during this whole war, even though your chariot was hit by a million missiles and bombs, it never exploded? It's because Hanuman absorbed all of those strikes."

There's another time when Hanuman comes to meet Krishna, and Krishna states, "Oh, I know what you want," and turns himself into Ram. Hanuman was monogamous, you know what I mean? He never looked at another avatar.

It turns out that I was quite all right with being called Krishna Das.

ᛁᛗ ᛚᛁᛗᛉᛗᚼᛁᚾ ᛉᛚᚼ ᛏᛁᛑ

Sometimes Maharaj-ji's lila was jaw-dropping in scope. There are moments when we know with total certainty that what happens really has nothing to do with us and the decisions we think we make in life. I'd been with Ram Dass and a group of other Westerners in Bodh Gaya in the fall of 1970. (Bodh Gaya is the place in India where Buddha sat under a tree and got enlightened.) We'd done five 10-day vipassana meditation courses in a row and felt that it was time to try to find Maharaj-ji again. Someone arrived in Bodh Gaya driving a Mercedes tour bus, and he offered the group a ride back to Delhi. We decided to go to Delhi to try to find out where Maharaj-ji might be.

It was a long day's drive to Delhi. One of the other Westerners on the bus had been to the *mela* (a large gathering at a holy spot at an astrologically prime time) in Allahabad and told us, "You know, there are millions of babas and sadhus taking their bath in the river at this holy place. Why don't we stop there? It's on the way." If we did stop at the mela, the chances of making it to Delhi that night weren't good, so Ram Dass didn't want to do it. And Ram Dass, being the eldest, was the boss.

This began a huge debate, with everybody on the bus saying what they wanted to do. For a long time Ram Dass was adamant about not stopping, but finally he gave in. "Okay, we'll go there and see the place for a few minutes, but then we'll get back on the bus and go."

As we pulled into this big field at the end of the road where the mela had taken place, we found it to be deserted. The ten million people who'd been there about ten days before had all gone home. So the bus was making a huge, long turn through this field to get back to the road when somebody said, "There's the Hanuman temple over there—why don't we go bow to Hanuman and then leave?"

The bus turned toward the temple and was driving alongside a footpath at the edge of the field when another person shouted out, "Look, there's Maharaj-ji!" And sure enough, he was walking in the opposite direction, kind of laughing to himself. He didn't even look up at the bus as it went by. Later the man he was walking with, who turned out to be Dada, told us that Maharaj-ji had said, "Oh, they've come," as he kept walking. The bus stopped, and we all ran out to see him. He said, "Follow me, follow me." He got into a small cycle rickshaw with Dada, which took off through these little streets followed by this huge, shiny Mercedes bus with all of these crazy Westerners on it.

We followed him to a house where he got off the rickshaw and went inside. We didn't know what to do. While we were standing by the bus, Dada's wife came out of the house and said, "Come, come in and take your food. This morning Maharaj-ji told us to prepare food for 26 people." There were 25 of us plus the driver. We had a great meal and a wonderful time with Maharaj-ji at this house. It was my first meeting with Dada, with whom I'd spend much time as the years went on.

My mind went back over the events of the last two days and all of the planning about the trip to Delhi to find Maharaj-ji.

I thought back over the long discussion about whether or not to stop at the mela. If I could have really understood, I would have seen that he was running the show and perhaps my mind would have surrendered. I often think that if I'd been ready, if I'd been ripe, this miracle would have been enough to melt my fickle mind forever!

On the bus, searching for Maharaj-ji, 1971. *(Courtesy of Jagganath Das.)*

When Maharaj-ji left Dada's house in Allahabad, a number of us decided to tour the south of India with Swami Muktananda until we could meet up with Maharaj-ji again. Maharaj-ji had told Ram Dass that he'd meet him in Brindavan, so we stopped there en route. Maharaj-ji wasn't there, so we continued south to Ganeshpuri, Swami Muktananda's ashram near Bombay. After doing a pilgrimage for a few weeks and visiting many holy sites with Swami Muktananda, we headed back up north to find Maharaj-ji. We were aiming for the mountains and Nainital, but remembering what Maharaj-ji had said, we thought there might be a chance that he'd be in Brindavan. So we made a detour. Just short of Brindavan, we stopped for the night at Krishna's birthplace, Mathura, where there was a good guesthouse. In the morning we headed to Brindavan, which was only a half hour down the road.

I was driving and somehow missed a turn, so we had to make a circle through the busy bazaar. It took an extra 20 minutes to reach the temple.

We arrived at the temple to find it deserted. The *chaukidhar* (watchman) said that Maharaj-ji wasn't there, nor did he have any idea where he was. We were all bitterly disappointed, and I hung my head as we got back into the car. Just as I was about to turn the key, a small car screeched to a halt right in front of us and Maharaj-ji got out. Without even a glance in our direction, he walked right in front of us and into the temple, leaving us sitting in the car with our minds blown!

Many years later, in 1989, I went to the Kumbh Mela in Allahabad. While visiting Maharaj-ji's camp, I met Gurudatt Sharma, the devotee with whom Maharaj-ji had arrived that day in Brindavan. We started reminiscing, and I asked if he remembered their sudden arrival that day. He remembered it perfectly and narrated his experience:

"I was with Maharaj-ji at a devotee's house in Lucknow. It was night, and most of the devotees had been sent back to their homes. I'd just fallen asleep when I heard him call for me in a loud voice. We sat together for some time, then he sent me to sleep. When I'd dozed off, I again heard him calling and went to him. Although I was in a room with several other devotees, no one else woke up.

"He said, 'I'm not feeling sleepy. Let's chat.' So we chatted for a while, then I was sent to sleep. Just as I fell asleep for a third time, I heard him call. As I reached him, he grabbed my hand and said *'Chalo* [Let's go].' We woke the driver and were soon on the road. All through the night, Maharaj-ji had the driver go at a breakneck speed. Then right outside of Brindavan, we stopped and sat by the side of the road for about 20 minutes, until he once again gave the order to move. When we got to the temple, I was walking with him, so I didn't know that you were even there until you came inside."

It was a lila with exquisite timing.

74

HAPPINESS AND
BUDDHA-NATURE

Maharaj-ji's presence awakened a feeling of well-being in me that I either had never known before, or had totally lost touch with. It took me many years to realize that it wasn't dependent on being with him physically but was there inside of me all along. In his book *Going on Being,* the Buddhist psychiatrist Mark Epstein writes about the tremendous importance of recognizing this inner well-being, and he illustrates it by telling the story of the Buddha.

Following the teachings that were available to him at the time, the Buddha-to-be had been doing such intense practices that he was basically starving himself to death. His austerity was so severe that when he went to scratch himself, his skin would come off, and when he went to the bathroom, he would fall over and not be able to get up for long periods of time. Feeling that he was close to death, he thought, *I can't do any harder practice, and yet I haven't found what I'm looking for. Could there be another way to enlightenment?*

Just at that moment he remembered a time when he was a boy, sitting in the cool shade of a tree as his father worked nearby. At that time, quite spontaneously, with no effort, he'd entered into a

ive state of deep happiness. As the memory of this warm,
state flooded him, he wondered, *Might this be the way to enlightenment?* He investigated the nature of the happy feeling and saw that it didn't come from outside of himself, nor did it come from the cessation of some painful experience. He recognized that this kind of pleasure was a quality of things as they are, that this feeling of well-being was natural, and innate to our true nature.

If such happiness is natural, what has happened to us? Why are we not in touch with that simple happiness? Why do we run around trying to fill this imagined void in ourselves that never seems to be satisfied?

When the Buddha came out of the jungle after his awakening, he was very clear about the fact that no matter what we do, where we go, or who we are, there will always be the presence of dissatisfaction in life. "Yo, monks! Stuff don't work!" That's what Buddha said, although he phrased it differently. And guess what? Stuff is not *supposed* to work. It's *stuff*. Stuff gives us pleasure, but pleasure doesn't last. It also has another side to it: pain. When pleasure's over, there's pain. When pain's over, there's pleasure. That's the way it works. We cling to the pleasure and try to push away the pain, but they're two sides of the same coin.

Growing up, I can't remember one person in my family who was happy. None of my relations were at ease with themselves or at peace with their life. Actually, there was one: Aunt Bella, who died when I was still very young. I met her only once or twice, but whenever her name came up, it was immediately followed by "Oh, she was a saint." Basically, what qualified her to be called a saint was that she was the only one in the history of my family who never complained. You know the joke of the two old Jewish ladies at a deli and the waiter comes over and asks, "So ladies, is *anything* all right?"

 The bottom line is that we find our path by following what makes us feel good. Why does that seem like such a revolutionary concept? Why do we spend so much time not doing what we want to do and complaining about what we wind up doing? If we follow our sense of well-being, if we follow our *heart* and do what makes us happy, it's going to lead us in the right direction.

Once I asked Sri Siddhi Ma, to whom Maharaj-ji had left the running of his temples and the care of his devotees, "Ma, should I meditate?"

She said, "You know, in all of the years I was with Maharaj-ji, he never once asked me to meditate. He said that meditation is not something we do willfully; it is a state we enter into naturally over time through devotion and the repetition of the Name." Then she asked, "What do you like to do, sing or meditate?"

I thought, *Well, I like to sing.*

The funny thing is that it never occurred to me that chanting, which I liked to do, was good for me in a deep, spiritual way. Why? Because I liked to do it. It brought up the whole issue of trusting myself. "Because I like it, it couldn't be good for me"—that's what my mother taught me! The problem is that our Western culture tends to completely destroy our ability to trust our own intuition. Nobody tells us to trust ourselves when we're kids. But developing that ability to know what truly moves us in a positive direction, and then *follow* that, is what this whole path is about. Because that place, that feeling of *rightness,* leads deeper and deeper into the place where *everything* is right, which is God, our true Self. We *are* it. We've forgotten that, so we're very busy trying to find it again.

> *The fish in the water*
> *is racked by thirst:*
> *I hear about it*
> *and burst out laughing.*
>
> *What you're looking for*
> *is right at home:*
> *and yet you roam from forest to forest,*
> *full of gloom . . .*

— Kabir[13]

Are we getting what we want from life? Is there enough love in our lives? Are we becoming good human beings? Do we feel connected to people, or are we isolated and afraid? Whatever the answers are to these questions, the issue that everything hinges on is: Do we really believe that there is a path to follow that will bring change? If not, then we're stuck where we are. Like a poor person who lives in a hut built above a buried treasure, we're limited by what we believe about ourselves.

Our belief systems change in two ways. The first is that we come into contact with something or someone that, spiritually, seems to have what we're looking for. We get a hit from that person or thing and then we can begin to look. The other way is that our own unhappiness gets so massive that we can no longer bear the pain. Something has to be done. This forces us out of the prison of our own beliefs to look for a way to put out the fire.

Once a music magazine was interviewing me. The interviewer asked what I thought about the big rock stars who were doing yoga and meditation—did I think it was just a fad? I replied, "No. It's exactly the opposite. These are the kings and queens of this world. They have the power to satisfy their desires to an extent that is beyond our wildest dreams. If they're doing yoga, chanting, and meditating, it's because they have gone to the furthest limit of fulfilling their desires and have had the direct personal experience that it isn't enough." This is real wisdom. These rock stars have taken it to the extreme and, for some of them, true wisdom has dawned. I think that this is extraordinary.

As we progress on the path, our understanding of happiness changes, as does our understanding of who we are and how we relate to other beings. The true results of doing spiritual practice are realized in our everyday lives. We become kinder and less fearful—more caring human beings. The desire to help others arises. We have to *have* happiness in order to share happiness. If we don't do the things that make us happy, how are we going to help anybody? A *bodhisattva* is one who's realized the interconnectedness of all beings and has vowed to remain in the world to work for the freedom of all. He knows that there's no freedom for an individual—no ultimate freedom—until all beings are free. He feels the pain of others as his own and does what he can to alleviate that suffering. He has found the deepest happiness within and wants only that we all share it.

This profound state is available to all of us . . . and that's the whole point.

> *Who burns with the bliss*
> *And suffers the sorrow*
> *of every creature in his own heart,*
> *Making his own*
> *Each bliss and each sorrow:*
> *him I hold as the highest Yogi . . .*

— from the Bhagavad Gita

Our problem is that we have bad aim. We launch ourselves in the wrong direction in our search for this elusive happiness. As long as we keep clinging to stuff in the hopes that it will bring us happiness, there will always be suffering involved. Every saint who has ever lived has told us to look inside. As Jesus said, "The kingdom of God is within." Real happiness, which comes from within, doesn't have another side. Happiness—true love—is what we *are*. It's Buddha Nature. Our True Being. Anything outside of us has to go away. Who we really are never comes and never goes. The better our sense of direction, the easier we'll be able to get where we're headed.

The way to enlightenment, the way to true happiness, is through the feeling of well-being that lives within us. Every day in India I'd get dressed and go sit with Maharaj-ji, and I'd wait to have my big enlightenment experience. I'd seen some of his close Indian devotees, like Gurudatt Sharma, or K.C. Tewari, go into *samadhi* (a very deep state of consciousness) while they were sitting there with him, or while singing to him, but nothing ever happened to me.

Nothing ever happened! He'd look at me and giggle and make me laugh and throw fruit, and I kept waiting for the big *boom!*

Then one day it struck me how ridiculous my idea of enlightenment was. I was waiting for him to touch me, for something to happen, and then *I* would be gone. I couldn't imagine that enlightenment, or happiness, would include my being there. I kept waiting to disappear, and that never happened. Still hasn't happened. How could it? I saw that the truth is exactly the opposite. There is no time or place where we will *not* be, ever. The absolute Divine Presence is in our hearts. *It* is always *here.*

On some level, we all know what that feels like or we wouldn't be looking for it. Spiritual practice that's done in the right spirit will increase that feeling of well-being. We have to learn how to feed that place inside ourselves. There's no other way to go. There's no other direction in which to find that love, to be in that presence. Everything else is just out *there.* We can use the world around us to make us feel good, and we can get very proficient at that, but if that is all we know, it's not enough. When we aim at the source of all, the inner Being, then everything that we need will come to us. Everything will get fulfilled over time. As Maharaj-ji always said, *"Ram Naam karne se, sab pura hojata.* [By repeating the name of Ram (God), everything is brought to completion.]"

I've taken teachings with a Tibetan *lama* (teacher) who's taught many Westerners. He noted that we Westerners as a rule are not in touch with this inner sense of well-being. We don't allow ourselves to simply feel okay about ourselves. Regular spiritual practice helps us get the strength to release the stuff that happens in our daily lives that makes us unhappy. All of the betrayals, all of the times we've been turned away, or pushed away, or hurt, or not gotten what we've wanted, or gotten what we didn't want—all of that stuff stays with us, sticks with us. In order to let go, we have to find something to hold on to that's deeper than all of that stuff. This is how we can make our hearts *available.* If we're afraid of being hurt, we won't allow ourselves to engage with life.

Ultimately, we'll come to live in a state where our hearts are so expansive, so open to love, that everyone and anything is free to come and go without being judged or pushed away. The Dalai Lama once said, "I guess you could say that I've had a hard life. I was forced to take political and spiritual charge of my country at a very young age. And I've had to watch as millions of my people have suffered and died from Chinese oppression. But I'm happy." And after an attack on his people by the Chinese, he described his feelings like this: "There are disturbing thoughts in the mind, but my heart is steady." It didn't destroy him or his peace of mind. In spite of everything that's happened to him and his people and his country—millions of people slaughtered, his country lost—he can say, "But I'm happy." He has the kind of happiness and peace that doesn't come or go, that doesn't depend on external things. That's a different kind of happiness. And he assures us that we can have it also.

॥ ॐ नमो भगवते वासुदेवाय ॥

In the winter of 1971, we were in Brindavan with Maharaj-ji. The other Westerners and I were staying at a guesthouse that was clean and cheap and not too far from the temple. My room had a window that faced the street. Every morning I'd be awakened by a blind sadhu as he passed by, singing *Radhe Radhe Radhe Shyam, Govinda Radhe Radhe!* (I had no idea that many years later, I would be recording CDs and would include a version of this very tune!)

On the way back to the guesthouse from the temple one night, I stepped into a hole in the road and snapped my knee. When I woke up in the morning, it was swollen and very painful. I figured that I should go to the hospital in Mathura and get it looked at.

Our instructions at the time were not to come to the temple for darshan until four o'clock in the afternoon, but if I was going to go to the hospital, I felt that I should tell Maharaj-ji before I went. So one of my *gurubhais* (guru-brothers) helped me get to the temple. I was limping and leaning on him as we walked across the back courtyard. Maharaj-ji was sitting on a takhat with only one devotee, Gurudatt Sharma, with him. We sat down, and I stretched my leg out straight under the takhat, not being able to bend at the knee. Maharaj-ji didn't ask why we'd come early, so I didn't say anything. I was just happy to be with him.

After a few minutes, Maharaj-ji got up and started to walk away from the takhat. Gurudatt was holding his hand. The farther away from us he got, the more he leaned on Gurudatt. With every step he began to limp more and more, as if he could hardly walk. I suddenly realized, *He's taking on the karma of my knee!* At that very instant, he turned around and hurried back to the takhat. He sat down, looked at me, and said, "You thought I was in pain? You wanted to help me?" And he patted me on the head.

After a while, he noticed the notebook in which I wrote down quotes and stories from holy books. He took it and started going through the pages. There were quotes from many different traditions: Hindu, Christian, Sufi, Buddhist. He stopped on one page and asked, "What's this?" I got very embarrassed. It was a hymn from the Tibetan Buddhist tradition—the "Song of Mahamudra" by the Mahasiddha Tilopa. *Mahamudra* literally means "the great gesture or symbol" and represents the union between a seeker and the universe. Buddhists don't believe in "God," and here I was in a temple dedicated to Hanuman, the monkey god. I felt like I'd gotten caught with my finger in the spiritual pie or something. I sheepishly said, "It's Buddhist."

Maharaj-ji said, "Translate it for me." So Gurudatt, who spoke perfect English, translated the first few verses. Maharaj-ji stopped him and said, "*Thik.* [Right. Correct.]" I couldn't believe it!

He kept leafing through the pages and came upon a picture of himself. He asked, "Who is this?"

"Maharaj-ji, it's you."

"*Nahin.* [No.] It's Buddha!" Then he closed the book and gave it back to me.

I was completely confused and had no understanding of what he was saying.

Later in the day, we were all sitting around with him. I was upset about my knee and obsessing about why I'd hurt it and what it could mean. Maharaj-ji was talking about my knee and telling everyone that I'd hurt it. He took my book again and went through it and picked out a different quote (by the way, he supposedly couldn't read English):

> And lest I should be exalted above measure through the abundance of the revelations, there was given me a thorn in the flesh. . . . For this thing, I besought the Lord thrice, that it might depart from me. And he said unto me, "My grace is sufficient for thee, for My strength is made perfect in weakness" (2 Corinthians 12:7–9).

To me, this meant that it's in our simple humanness that the strength and beauty of that Divine Love can shine. We don't have to be special or "exalted" in the world to receive that grace.

Years later, Dr. Larry Brilliant and his wife, Girija, were in Sikkim. Larry and Girija were other Western devotees, and through Maharaj-ji's prodding, Larry was working for the United Nations' World Health Organization on the project that actually wiped out smallpox in the world. While in Sikkim, Larry and his wife went to have darshan of His Holiness, the 16th Karmapa, the head of the Kagyu Lineage of Tibetan Buddhism, who was recognized as one the great saints in the world. The Karmapa asked about their spiritual practice, and they showed him a picture of Maharaj-ji.

The Karmapa looked at Maharaj-ji's photo and said, "He is a bodhisattva. For sure he is a bodhisattva. Just as Chenrezig (Avalokitesvara) is a bodhisattva, he is a bodhisattva. The teachings of all bodhisattvas are the same, even if they appear different. He is a *Mahasiddha*." The Karmapa pointed to statues on his altar and said, "These are Tibetan statues of Mahasiddhas." He asked Kongtrul Rinpoche to explain to Dr. Larry and Girija about Mahasiddhas. A Mahasiddha is a Great Being who has attained the highest state of perfection, often through the practice of Mahamudra. The prayer that Maharaj-ji had pointed to in my notebook was "The Song of Mahamudra."

H.H. Karmapa said to them, "I can't give you what your guru can give you, but I can offer you refuge," referring to the Buddhist practice of taking refuge in the triple gem: Buddha, dharma, and sangha. When Larry and Girija asked if they could take refuge without leaving their guru, H.H. Karmapa said that they didn't have to leave their guru. They could take refuge in Neem Karoli Baba instead of Buddha!

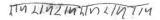

THE FRUIT OF
ATTACHMENT IS TEARS

$$\overline{\mathcal{H} \upsilon \, \mathcal{H} \, \mathcal{V}}$$

At the beginning of winter in 1972, Maharaj-ji was staying at Dada's house in Allahabad. My guru-brothers and I were staying nearby and would visit every day. It was a time when Ram Dass and many of the other American devotees had to get their visas extended, which was very difficult to do. When someone told them that there was an official in Delhi they could bribe, the whole group decided to go there. They told Maharaj-ji the plan, and he let them go. As it turned out, they were all ordered to leave India immediately and couldn't come back to Brindavan to see Maharaj-ji again.

My visa also had to be extended. But because I'd already gotten one extension, I had to go back to the same office in the town of Gaya and couldn't go to Delhi. I brought my bags to Dada's house and told him of my plans to leave that night for Gaya. I asked if I could see Maharaj-ji first. Just before I had to leave for the train, Dada came out of Maharaj-ji's room and told me not to go. Maharaj-ji told Dada that he would send me to a devotee of his who was chief of police in a large city and that he'd arrange for my visa extension. So I stayed in Allahabad.

When Maharaj-ji learned that Ram Dass and the other devotees had had to leave India, he made a big deal about it, telling everyone, "Oh, Ram Dass and the others tried to go to the highest level, and they were sent home. But Krishna Das was so humble, he got to stay in India." The reality, of course, was that I didn't go to Delhi because I had to go to the original office. Otherwise, I would have been sent home like the others.

After some time, Maharaj-ji left Allahabad to travel to South India. I was in a strange in-between space. My time in India up until this point had been spent mostly with the Westerners who'd just been sent back to America, and I found myself alone. I made my way up to foothills of the Himalayas, the beautiful Kumaon hills that always felt like home to me. I figured that I'd stay up there and wait for Maharaj-ji to return to Kainchi in the spring. It felt like one part of my life was over, but I didn't know what was coming next. It was exhilarating yet a little scary as well.

There was a small hut in an orchard about 15 miles outside of Nainital that was then owned by K.K., which many saints had stayed in over the years. After receiving K.K.'s permission to stay there myself for a couple of weeks, I went out to the hut with a whole bunch of supplies: powdered milk, rice, and *dal* (lentils). I would be left alone because they respected that I wanted to do a retreat. On the first evening, I made my tea and watched the sun set over the vast plains of India. It was completely magical. I could hear the children calling to each other across the valley, and the sound of dogs barking floated in the air. The light was soft and beautiful. I went to sleep very happy.

I woke in the middle of the night with chills, which changed to burning fever and then chills again, all night long. By the time morning came, I didn't have the strength to get up, so I lay there until I finally realized, *This is not particularly cool. Nobody's coming to see me for a long time, and I can barely move. What am I going to do?* With the pure logic of delirium, I decided to roll myself down the hill to the road. Since I couldn't walk, I dragged myself out of the hut, and then I threw one shoulder over the other until I reached the bottom of the hill. I lay in a ditch on the side of the road all day long. Cars would occasionally come and go, but nobody saw me. The sun began to set, and it started to get cold. It was early March and still very cold at night, especially where I was, at about 5,000 feet. I realized that if I continued to lie there and nobody picked me up, I would freeze to death.

What to do? There was no other option but to roll out into the middle of the road so that I could be seen. There was a slight incline, and at the bottom the road curved, so I couldn't see what was coming up the hill until it was very close. Lying there with my face pressed against the road and no strength to move, I felt the vibration of a big vehicle laboring up the hill. Sure enough, a big blue government bus came around the bend. As it got closer to me, I wondered if it was going to roll right over me. It came to a stop about ten feet from my head, and everybody piled off to see what was going on. They picked me up and laid me down on the floor of the bus. When we arrived in town, a little Nepali bearer carried me on his back like a sack of potatoes through the bazaar and up the stairs to K.K.'s house. I didn't leave for more than two months while recovering from what turned out to be a very bad case of hepatitis.

At one point during this time, some Western devotees came to see me from Brindavan, where they'd been staying with Maharaj-ji after his return from his trip down south. Since they were going back, I sent a note with them to Maharaj-ji, thanking him for everything and saying that I'd see him in my next life. I was so sick that I really thought I might die, but in the state I was in, I didn't care.

My friends wrote to me from Brindavan to say that all Maharaj-ji did when he read my note was to laugh and say, "*Sab thik hojaega.* [Everything will be all right.]" He also asked them if I'd received a letter from the U.S. and if I was married. I hadn't, and I wasn't.

Right after this, I did in fact get a letter from an old friend in the States. She told me that my ex-girlfriend, Gail, was in a mental hospital on Long Island after trying to starve herself to death on a commune in Vancouver. This friend had visited Gail in the hospital, and Gail had asked about me. This surprised me, as we'd had a very messy breakup years before. Two days before I was to leave for India, I tried to track her down and smooth things over before I went on to what I felt would be a new life, but I couldn't find her. It wasn't meant to be.

As I lay there in my little dark corner at K.K.'s, holding the letter and thinking about Gail, I began to fantasize about going back to the States to help her, even thinking that I'd marry her. Soon another letter arrived from the States, saying that Gail had escaped from the hospital, had thrown herself in front of a Long Island Rail Road train, and was dead. *Dead!* It hit me hard. I realized that because it had taken two weeks for the first letter to reach me, Gail had already died before I got it. This was a big shock. I realized that the best thing I could do was ask for Maharaj-ji's blessings for her when I saw him again.

Some weeks passed, and I got stronger day by day. Then the news came: Maharaj-ji had returned to the hills! There was one subtle but interesting difference for me. While Ram Dass had been in India, Maharaj-ji called him Commander in Chief; as our elder gurubhai, he was in charge of the "troops." Since Ram Dass and many of the Westerners I was close to had left India, I arrived at the temple by myself on my first day back at Kainchi. I went up to the takhat and bowed to Maharaj-ji, then I went to sit across the courtyard from him, as we'd always done when Ram Dass was there.

After about 20 minutes, I began to feel strange sitting there alone, so far away from Maharaj-ji. I looked around to see if anyone was watching and hesitantly made my way across the courtyard. I was very self-conscious, so when I sat down close to Maharaj-ji, I stared at the ground. After a few minutes, I slowly looked up at him, expecting him to send me back across the courtyard. He was talking to some Indian devotees and gave no indication that there was anything unusual about my sitting there. I was beginning to listen to what my own heart was telling me, and I began to develop a deeper, more intimate relationship with him.

Although I was still physically weak, I was so happy to see Maharaj-ji again that I forgot all about Gail. I was also feeling emotionally raw and having many intense dreams. Maharaj-ji began a daily program of asking me if I wanted to get married, which made me very uneasy. My policy had been to do nothing that could ever give Maharaj-ji the opportunity to send me away. I'd seen so many of my guru-brothers and -sisters get turned on to each other—and then the next thing they knew, they had, in Maharaj-ji's words, become *friends*. From then on, every day he would laugh and ask them, "Are you friends? Yes, you're friends now. Will you get married? Yes, you're married now. Jao! Go to America, see your parents." "Friends" had become a ticket to the States and away from him.

There was no doubt that after a year and a half of being celibate, my mind was on fire with sexual fantasies, but this fire was constantly being consumed by the greater blaze of his love. Back and forth I swung, from the crazed, lustful fantasies in my mind to the peaceful, sweet refuge in his heart. The intensity was building daily, and I was in total despair of ever getting beyond it. The fact that I judged myself so harshly for my feelings made life unbearable.

A week or so after Maharaj-ji returned to Kainchi, I had a dream about Gail. She and I were walking down the road that went by the house I grew up in. I was feeling very calm and loving toward her, yet she was completely insane and hissed at me: "Why didn't you help me?" I spoke to her as if I were talking her down from a really bad acid trip. When we reached my mother's house, for some reason I left her standing in the road and went inside. The sound of the door closing behind me woke me up. I was sweating and shaking and feeling her in the room. *She'd almost made it all the way back; why did I leave her on the road?* I was so freaked-out that I didn't sleep the rest of the night.

In the morning, I ran to the temple as early as I could and told Maharaj-ji the whole story of Gail—how she died and the dream. As Dada translated the story into Hindi, Maharaj-ji closed his eyes and slowly rocked back and forth. He then told me, "Two days before she died, she thought of you; she wanted to see you. That is why this has come back to you now." He tapped me on the head and gave me his blessing, saying, "She won't disturb you anymore. She will be okay now. She will be okay." I asked him if she'd have a good birth next time, and he said that she would. Then he said that she'd divorced me, and he asked if I felt bad about the death of my wife.

"No," I replied, "everyone must die. But it does upset me that she suffered so much."

Then he looked at me and asked, "Why did you leave her?"

I was stunned by the question. I said, "I was very young then . . . and actually, she left me." As I was saying this, my mind cleared, and I realized that I'd been lying to myself all of these years. What had really happened was that I'd pulled back from her emotionally, so she'd found another boyfriend. But I was ashamed and couldn't say anything. He kept asking, "What do people feel when someone dies?" Then he sent me outside.

The next day, K.K. and the whole extended Sah family came to Kainchi for their yearly puja to Maharaj-ji. We all crowded into the room to watch. After the puja, they offered a blanket to him. Sometimes when Maharaj-ji accepted a new blanket, he'd remove the one he was wearing and give it to a devotee. As he took his blanket off, my mind ignited with lust for it. I wanted that blanket more than anything in the world. He put on the new blanket and threw the old one to another Western devotee who was sitting right next to me. I heard a crack of thunder: my mind had snapped. The thin thread that had been holding me together throughout the whole drama with Gail and the repeated questions from Maharaj-ji about getting married and how someone feels when people die—and the fact that I was not ready to see so much of my shit—all combined to explode in my head.

Maharaj-ji heard it, too. He immediately turned to me and said, "Read the Bhagavad Gita. Read the Gita." He pointed to the guy who'd gotten the blanket and said, "Give Krishna Das a Gita."

After leaving the room, I was like a planet that had broken free from its orbit and was sailing out into space. I was completely lost in a fit of panic, guilt, and anger. I saw that K.K.'s family was about to leave to return to Nainital, and I thought that I'd escape with them. As I passed through the door in the wall that separated the back of the temple from the front, Maharaj-ji was waiting for me at his window. I'd been caught.

"Where are you going?" he asked.

"I want to go to Nainital with the Sahs."

"Why?"

"I got upset this morning, and I feel too impure and filled with desires. I want to be alone."

"Do you remember the girl who died much?"

"No."

"Don't go. Your desires will be bigger in loneliness and will overpower you. Stay with people and your desires will be subdued." Then he asked if I wanted to marry one of the Western women in the group.

"No."

"Go sit in the back."

I did.

Later in the evening, Maharaj-ji looked at me and said, "Don't be alone. Sit with people." He told me again to read the Bhagavad Gita. I opened the Gita, and my eyes fell on this verse:

> *Their soul is warped with selfish desires,*
> *And their heaven is a selfish desire.*
> *They have prayers for pleasures and power,*
> *The reward of which is earthly rebirth.*

I couldn't believe it! More salt in the wound. Every part of me was screaming in pain.

The next day, I was reading again from the Bhagavad Gita, the section where Sri Krishna says to Arjuna, "The soul isn't born. It doesn't die." The book fell from my hands. As I stared at the floor, a black hole appeared and turned into a dark whirlpool cloud that was pulling me down into it. Just as I was beginning to disappear into the hole, one of my gurubhais came into the room, and in a quiet, shaky voice, said, "Krishna Das, Maharaj-ji is calling for you." (Ten years later I was sitting in a restaurant in Berkeley, California, with the same devotee. He said, "Did I ever tell you what Maharaj-ji really said that day? 'Quick! Go get Krishna Das before he kills himself!'") The pull into the black whirlpool was broken.

As I moved in a dreamlike state toward the front of the temple where Maharaj-ji was sitting, I began to cry. By the time I reached him, I had totally lost it and was sobbing uncontrollably. I collapsed at his feet. Sitting there, my head bowed down with the weight of a sorrow I'd never felt before, I cried and cried. I felt as if my lifeline had run out. I simply could not see a future.

I became aware of Maharaj-ji sitting above me on the takhat, completely still. His silence held me like the soft arms of a mother. He didn't try to stop my weeping, but within the roar of these terrible waves of anguish crashing over me, I heard his silent whisper calling to my soul. He began to speak, slowly and simply. My joking, laughing guru was gone; in his place was Krishna, the divine charioteer, slowly gathering up the threads of his fallen devotee's life.

As my tears finally ran out, he gently began to talk about Gail, saying that I shouldn't grieve over her. He reminded me, "The soul isn't born. It doesn't die" . . . quoting the very part of the Gita that I'd been reading.

"Why are you crying?" he asked.

"I can't serve you purely. I'm full of desires and think only of my own happiness, never of others. I'm so selfish—"

He cut me off midsentence. "Attachment! This is all attachment! You're crying because of attachment. All of these thoughts are the result of attachment. The fruit of lust, anger, greed, and attachment is tears. You are reaping that fruit now. This is wisdom develops."

"How can I understand these things within myself and break attachment?"

"Think of Jesus. He gave his life for his people, his country, and humanity. He could have married and had a family, but then he wouldn't have been Christ. He never thought of himself, or his life or death, so he couldn't die like a worldly person. He became immortal. The death of worldly people isn't real death. You can die only if you don't think of yourself."

Later, one of the Indian devotees explained to me that "the soul is born once and dies when it is merged in God. Many bodies come and go, but they're like suits of clothes that are worn and thrown away." As I understand it, a saint like Jesus dies to his small self, so, in essence, even if he offers his body as a sacrifice for others, he doesn't die like a worldly person; he merges with God. However, when a worldly person's body dies, he doesn't die the real death of the ego, the "death" of merging in God.

Maharaj-ji continued, "The body is perishable! This is not something to be dimly known, it is *absolutely true*. When you realize that the body is perishable, you don't think about throwing it in a river because you know that it is completely unreal. When a cloth is torn, you cast it away and don't feel bad. When a body dies, it's the same thing. No one can die for another. Everyone must die alone. When someone dies, everyone cries and moans and grieves, but in a few days they're eating and drinking and making merry, as if nothing happened. Why be attached? No one else would die for you. It's all the play of attachment."

"I don't want to get married before I feel inside that it will be good and not lead me away from God."

"That time will come. These memories will pass. One set of attachments is replaced by another, on and on. One day you're sad about something, but you forget what was upsetting you, only to be involved in a whole new set of attachments. When you wake from a dream, you see that it's empty and you forget about it; you don't take the dream as real or try to hold on to it. That's the way the world is. All of the world is a dream: a lie, a lie, a lie. Why be attached to it? All of creation is the result of attachment. If all attachment was gone, there would be no world! Both attachment and its eradication are acts of God."

Then Maharaj-ji quoted Kabir: "Illusion doesn't die, nor does the mind / Even though so many of your bodies have died / Hope doesn't die, nor does thirst, so says Kabir."

I blurted out, "I'm so full of pride. I always think of myself. What can I do with my life?"

He looked at me and cracked up, chiding me in his own sweet way, "What will you do? Jump in the river? Ha! You can't kill yourself. Worldly people don't die."

"Will I ever get through these things?"

"Of course! You're already getting though them. That's what this explosion is all about. This suffering will pass like every other attachment passes. One attachment replaces another. This is why no one attachment is more real than another. When there is no *moha* [attachment], all is One." He bopped me on the head and said, "You'll be happy when you're married."

"Maharaj-ji," I said, "I want to marry you!"

He laughed, sat bolt upright, and slapped his thigh. "Now you're talking. But love and attachment are different. If you marry me, all you'll get is love. Your attachments won't get worked out, and you won't achieve the married state!"

He laughed and laughed, as the translator, a very proper Indian, blushed uncontrollably as he struggled to fit Maharaj-ji's gutter slang into his prim and proper British English. As the laughter died down, Maharaj-ji placed a flower on my head and gave me much prasad. In a matter-of-fact voice, he reminded me, "Even birds have attachment. Everything in a body has attachment. When you die, you can't take anything with you."

Whack! He smacked me on the head. "He's sad now, but he'll be happy when he's married!"

"I'm afraid that my desires will be too strong and I'll get lost in *samsara* [worldly life]."

He looked right at me and kind of threw up his hands: "So get married! It won't interfere with your ability to serve God purely. A man can be *brahmachari* [celibate] if he's constant with one woman for his whole life." He repeated over and over, "Two days before, two days before . . . two days before she passed, she thought of you. This is the reason that this attachment has come out. You'll have to get married again. Tears of joy of God are different from tears of attachment."

A devotee sitting there announced, "Maharaj-ji is my biggest attachment!"

Maharaj-ji said, "Now you're on the right track!"

He whacked me on the head again. "Now you're all right! Why don't you sleep at night? Why do you wander around? When you're married, you'll sleep."

I felt that my life had been given back to me. I felt his hand behind every event, directing all of the action, bringing all of these karmas to a head.

The next afternoon, I was sitting in the jungle on a rock and was still somewhat freaked-out. I went running to Maharaj-ji's "office" and peered through the window into the room. He drew himself up to the other side, and I asked, "Am I ever going to get through this stuff?"

He laughed and said, "*Thik hai,* it's okay, it's okay. It'll be all right . . . it's getting better now, everything's getting better. You're Hanuman, you wear red. You're Bajrangbali [another name for Hanuman]. What's your name?"

There was no way I could accept that name of Hanuman. *He* was Hanuman. So I said, "Krishna Das."

"No. Bajrangbali. What's your name?"

"Krishna Das."

"No! Bajrangbali."

"Okay. You want me to be Bajrangbali? No problem, but remember, Bajrangbali was eternally celibate."

He laughed so hard. Then he said, "Okay, okay, you're Janaka [in the Hindu epic of the *Ramayana*, Janaka is a wise king whose daughter, Sita, marries Lord Rama]. You'll have *yoga* [union with God] and *bhoga* [earthly pleasures]. Janaka was a *raja-rishi,* a king-saint, a *gyani,* a fully enlightened being; pleasure and pain, birth and death were one to him." He went on, "The lean times are over now. The good times will come. Now the good times will come . . . *sukh* [happiness] and *dukh* [suffering] are one. It's all God's will."

From that time on, I wore long red *ulfies* (robes)—the color of Hanuman. He ordered me to dye everything I had red, even my underwear!

THE MANY MOODS OF LOVE

$\overrightarrow{{\it{\!\!\!\!\!\!\!\!\!}}}$

No matter what trip I was going through, what flavor of my current neurosis, Maharaj-ji never got caught up in it. He didn't push me away either. With other human beings, we lay out our trips and certain people buy them . . . and then we have relationships. If someone doesn't buy our trip, we feel rejected. But with Maharaj-ji, there was no rejection, even though he didn't buy into our trips.

When I was growing up, I used illness to get attention—a strategy that worked in my family. So whenever I got sick in India, I unconsciously expected it to bring some kind of special attention from Maharaj-ji. While I was living in the temple with him and slowly recovering from hepatitis, I got a fever one day and thought, *Uh-oh, I'm having a relapse.* So I stayed in bed all day. Since I was seeing Maharaj-ji four or five times a day, I figured, *He'll ask about me.* I hoped that he was going to say, "Where is Krishna Das? What's going on? Is there something wrong?"

I lay in my room all day long waiting for somebody to tell me that Maharaj-ji asked about me, but the whole day went by and he never asked. So the next morning I got up and decided, *Well, I'll just go see him.* I still wasn't feeling very well. The minute he saw me from across the courtyard, he started shouting, "He's sick! Get him out of here! Take him right to the hospital! Get him out now!" Although I only wanted to go over and touch his feet, he wouldn't let me. Some devotees drove me to the hospital in Nainital, where a doctor examined me and took blood samples. They kept me there for a few days of recuperation, after which they said, "Your liver function is good now. You're okay."

Since I'd had a severe case of hepatitis, I'd only been eating dry toast, bananas, and other totally bland food for several months— no oil, no butter, no sugar, no spices, no greasy food. In India, that means there's hardly anything you can eat. When I left the hospital with a clean bill of health from the doctor, I went to the bus station to wait for the next bus back to the temple. I was sitting at a chai stand. I hadn't had any chai for ages, so I thought, *I got a clean bill of health. Why don't I have a cup of tea?*

As I was ordering, I noticed a huge pan full of *samosas* next to me. Samosas are triangular pockets of fried dough surrounding potatoes and vegetables. If you've eaten Indian food, you've probably had them. But you've never seen samosas like these, which were prepared at six in the morning with mustard oil, which is one grade lighter than motor oil, and they'd been soaking in the oil all day long. Each one looked like it weighed about 30 pounds. But since I was celebrating my good health, I ordered a plate of samosas and sat for a while in the tea stall drinking my chai and eating. I was in heaven.

I caught the bus back to the temple. It stopped in a little town along the way, where I bought some apples as prasad for Maharaj-ji. As I entered the temple, I found Maharaj-ji sitting alone. I walked over to his takhat, put the apples down, and bowed to him. As I looked up, he leaned over and scrunched up his face with mock anger. He said, "Samosas, *nahin!* [Don't eat samosas!]"

Stuff like that was always happening. And even though everyone around Maharaj-ji still had their usual programs running, he rarely said a word directly about any of it. Nevertheless, he still found ways to show us that he was completely aware of it and that it didn't matter to him, allowing us to become less identified with it. Despite the fact that Maharaj-ji knew every single thing about me, I never felt judged by him. I never felt that he saw me as unlovable. This kind of unconditional love is very hard to be around. We all *think* we want love. We *say* we want love, but we don't let it in. We have to invite love in. But where's the room? There are boxes and cartons piled high in our hearts with jealousy, anger, and self-hatred.

Once Ram Dass was extremely angry. Of course, Maharaj-ji had fanned the flames. Ram Dass stormed up to him and Maharaj-ji asked, "What's wrong?"

"I'm angry."

"Tell the truth and don't be angry," Maharaj-ji directed.

"The truth is that I'm angry and I don't love anybody."

"Tell the truth, love everybody, and don't be angry."

"I'm angry," Ram Dass stubbornly insisted. "I hate everybody. I'm so impure. I don't have any love."

Maharaj-ji made him stand up and turn around slowly. Then Maharaj-ji said, "I don't see any impurity." He saw purely and truly what we are: love. He had no trouble loving us or letting us love him.

जय जय सीताराम जय राम

In general, our hearts are only available if we get exactly the right stimulus in the right way from the right person at the right moment. The rest of the time, we're watching television or doing whatever else it is that we normally do. When we first fall in love with someone, everything she does seems wonderful and amazing. We can't take our eyes off of her for a minute. We think of her all the time. Then we begin to notice that she doesn't wash her dishes and she leaves dirty clothes all around. She starts acting in ways that hurt us and close us down. With Maharaj-ji, that never happened. But sometimes Maharaj-ji would appear to get angry . . . *really* angry.

One time we were sitting in the back of the temple with him and a man named Purnanand came in. He lived across the street from the ashram at Kainchi. Maharaj-ji had known him for a very long time; Purnanand was actually the first person Maharaj-ji had talked to when he came to that area, many years before. On this day, when Purnanand came into the back part of the temple, Maharaj-ji sat up and started hollering at the top of his lungs. We were all sitting there, totally flabbergasted. With every step Purnanand took, Maharaj-ji screamed with rage and anger. The man bowed down to Maharaj-ji, who started pounding him on the back and calling him every name in the book. "Get out! *Hap!*" And Purnanand ran.

When he was gone, Maharaj-ji giggled, *"Hee hee!"* His anger had just been part of the lila.

Later we found out the story. Purnanand had a huge family and didn't have a job, so Maharaj-ji had created a job for him with the government bus service. All he had to do was count the buses as they went by, and for that he got paid a certain amount of rupees every month, which allowed him to feed his family of 13. Earlier that day, he'd received his pay and spent it all on hashish, which he smoked all the time. So his family was going to starve for the next month. Maharaj-ji *knew* all that, and that's why he was screaming at Purnanand. Of course, Maharaj-ji fed this man's family for the next month, as he'd done many times before, and screamed at him again the following month when he did the same thing.

Another time, Dada was alone with Maharaj-ji. In the distance they heard the firing of guns from the Army rifle range. Dada began to laugh. Maharaj-ji asked him why he was laughing. Dada replied, "Because you're just like the Army."

"How so?"

"Always firing blanks!"

Maharaj-ji cracked up and agreed, "Yes, Dada, I *am* like the Army, just like the Army. Always firing blanks."

On rare occasions, Maharaj-ji got *very* quiet and still. One day at Kainchi, for instance, we were called from the room at the back of the temple where we spent a large part of the day banished to "inner darkness"—whenever we weren't in his presence, we felt like the sun had stopped shining. It was late afternoon, when we usually spent time with him before the last bus of the day came and we had to go back to Nainital. We poured into Maharaj-ji's room and settled in on the floor in front of his takhat. We sat quietly and looked at him in awe. In place of the joking, lighthearted guru we knew and loved, there was a living statue. He was unmoving, absorbed in some deep inner state, seemingly unaware of anything in the room. We were all deeply affected and sat there, silently, floating in his essence.

After a few minutes he opened his eyes and softly said, "Jao—go. Bus has come." His eyes closed again. Nobody in the room moved. It was as if we were rooted to the ground. Again, after a few minutes, his eyes opened and he softly repeated "Jao," but he disappeared within himself immediately. We kept sitting there, staring at the beauty and majesty of this Being. Wrapped in a blanket, sitting on a simple wooden bed, he seemed to be the very center of the universe. A few more minutes passed. I could barely breathe, yet it seemed as if there were no need for air. I was suspended in midspace; the earth and all of its gravity had disappeared.

Finally, someone couldn't stand it any longer and blurted out, "Maharaj-ji, what *is* this?"

That broke the mood. He was back fully, and with great intensity said, "It's in the blood. It's in the blood. *Jao! Go!*" Everyone was bowing, moving, and being swept out of the room, out of the temple, and into the bus that would haul us back to town.

Once when we were in Allahabad at Dada's house, I was sitting with the other devotees, waiting for Maharaj-ji. Thinking that he was in his room, I went out to wait on the porch. It was night, and as my eyes grew accustomed to the dim light, I saw that Maharaj-ji was all alone, sitting in a chair and looking out into the night. I walked up to him but he didn't look at me, so I sat down in front of him. I took his leg to massage it and, surprised, his head whipped around to see who was there. His eyes were wide open and lit with the fire of the state he'd been in before I interrupted him. There was no covering over them—nothing but pure, raw God—and for one second, his eyes burned into mine. I began to explode, but he instantly softened himself. Smiling at me, he said, "*Tik*. It's okay." Then he told me to go.

Instead of going back into the house, I staggered back to the place the other devotees and I were staying in, which was a short walk from Dada's. I got into my sleeping bag, still feeling the effects of that look. One of my gurubhais was reading out loud from a holy book called the Ashtavakra Gita and, as I passed into sleep, the last words I heard were:

On the ocean of consciousness,
The ship of the universe is blown about
By the winds of desire.
Let it come and go.
You're not affected by it.

I immediately entered a dream in which it was a Tuesday, Hanuman's day. I'd gone down to the ocean, and strolling along the shore, I found a boat waiting for me. I stepped into it and sat down. I had great faith in the boatman and was completely at ease. Slowly he guided the boat through the rough waves out to the open sea. As we headed out to the horizon, I sat and watched the moon starting to rise. Its light spread ecstatically, diffusing all around. We threw *laddus*, Hanuman's favorite sweets, into the ocean as an offering, and the gods accepted it.

The moon never rose completely over the horizon, but its light spread in silver blue concentric circles in all directions. It was actually not light, but silvery rays of bliss that entered me, over and over again, every second. The bliss was so intense that I was a little afraid. Something was holding me back from total absorption, yet it was the most powerful experience I had ever had. There seemed to be something left undone on this, the waking plane—some person or thing I wanted to hold on to, some desire, or something I wanted to know. I was very close to being able to surrender all of me, but not quite yet. I knew that the ship of my life was being totally guided. The feeling of being guided through the waves, of relaxing and letting go, was indescribable.

Then the scene changed. I was in bed reading the *Ramayana,* which immediately opened the channels to that earlier experience. In fact, I was reading about it in the book. I realized that this was the way to keep in touch with other planes of consciousness. I felt totally fulfilled and at ease in the world.

All of this came from one millionth-of-a-second glimpse of Maharaj-ji's Being.

He hid himself from the other devotees and me because we simply were not able to bear the radiance of his true Being. Dada used to say that Maharaj-ji had two blankets: a woolen one to cover his body and an inner one to cover his inner radiance. Great saints have to cover themselves because their light is too bright. We can't bear it—it's just too strong for us to be with them. They cover themselves with different veils so that we can *withstand* being in their presence. In the Bhagavad Gita, Arjuna freaked when Krishna showed him his true form; Arjuna begged him to shut it down and simply be his friend again.

Maharaj-ji knew exactly what we could take without disintegrating; he orchestrated everything perfectly . . . and continues to do so.

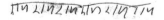

AMERICA

Just before Christmas in 1972, Maharaj-ji ran away again. No one knew where he'd gone. I had a feeling that he was somewhere with one of his Delhi devotees, J.L. Barman. Barman's driver seemed to know something, and a friend and I convinced him to tell us that his boss had gone to Bombay and was staying at the Nataraj Hotel, without saying whether Maharaj-ji was with him or not. My friend bought tickets, and we flew right to Bombay. We arrived at the hotel in the early afternoon and sat in the lobby.

After a few hours, Barman arrived and saw us there. "Krishna Das," he asked me, "what are you doing here?"

"Mr. Barman, we heard that Maharaj-ji was in Bombay."

"In Bombay! Really? I didn't know. I have to go out again on some business. Why not go up to my room and wash up and eat something? When I come back, we'll try to find him."

My friend and I indeed went upstairs and hung out in Barman's room. I couldn't believe that we had come all this way and didn't have anything to show for it. If Barman didn't know where Maharaj-ji was, how would we ever find him? I was looking out the window feeling miserable, when the door to the room opened and in walked Maharaj-ji, followed by Barman. Ecstasy!

My friend and I got rooms in the hotel, and Maharaj-ji would come and spend a few hours with us every day. It was so great, hanging out with him like that. Most of the time he'd just lie on the bed or chat with us. One day, however, I was sitting at the foot of the bed when Maharaj-ji sat up and said, really intensely, "Give me the seed. Give me the seed the lama gave you."

I had no idea what he was talking about. I replied, "Maharaj-ji, what seed?"

He repeated, "Give me the seed. Give me the seed."

I had met many great Tibetan lamas in India. *What seed was he talking about?* Then all of a sudden I remembered that about two years earlier, I'd been taking meditation courses in Bodh Gaya, in the village built around the tree where Buddha was enlightened, when I had the darshan of a greatly respected old lama named Khunu Rinpoche. He was the teacher of the Dalai Lama's teachers, as well as for His Holiness himself. He lived very humbly in a little room in the Tibetan *dharmasala* (housing unit). He was so beautiful and sweet. He gave us mantra and then, as we were about to leave, he reached into his *chuba* (robe) and pulled out an old leather bag. Reaching into it, he took out some seeds from the Bodhi tree and gave one to each of us. I was about to put mine away when he told me that I should eat it right away. So I did. Then we bowed and left the room.

I couldn't believe that Maharaj-ji was talking about this. I told him, "But Maharaj-ji, he made me eat it."

As he lay back down on the bed, Maharaj-ji said, "Very good. Now you'll be enlightened."

During our stay at the hotel, Maharaj-ji asked me to call the governor of Madhya Pradesh (a state in India). In those days, calls had to be booked with the operator and then you had to wait for a call back. After some time, the phone rang and I picked it up. There was someone from the governor's office on the line. I said, "I'm calling for Neem Karoli Baba. He would like to talk to the governor."

The man on the other end of the line responded haughtily, "I'm sorry, but the governor is not available." I said okay, hung up, and told Maharaj-ji what I'd been told. About 20 minutes later, Maharaj-ji got up and went into the bathroom. The minute he closed the door behind him, the phone rang. I picked it up and heard: "Hello, this is the governor of Madhya Pradesh. Can I speak to Maharaj-ji?"

I smiled to myself at Maharaj-ji's playfulness. "I'm sorry, Maharaj-ji is not available. You'll have to wait."

"Oh yes, I will wait. No problem," replied the governor.

As we both waited for Maharaj-ji, I realized how difficult it must have been for the governor to trace the call and how bad he wanted to speak to Maharaj-ji. After about 15 minutes, Maharaj-ji came out and had a nice chat with the governor.

We were still staying at the hotel on Christmas Eve, my father's birthday, so I booked a call to him. I hadn't spoken to him since I left America, almost two years earlier. When the call came through, we were very happy to talk together. Later that day I went to see Maharaj-ji. As I was bowing to him, he asked, "Do you think about your mother?"

"Sometimes."

"Do you think about your father?"

I got a sinking feeling in the pit of my stomach. "Sometimes. I telephoned him today."

"*Accha.* You go back to America. You have attachments there."

I was completely in shock. I didn't know what to say, so I stammered, "But Maharaj-ji, I'm just learning Hindi."

"Too bad. Go!"

Then he got up and went into the bathroom. I waited outside the door for him. As I stood there, I began to freak out about going back. I never thought about going back to America. *Ever.* He came out of the bathroom, took my hand, and without looking at me laughed. "Attachment!"

I laughed, too, and all of a sudden everything seemed okay. He told me that I should go back when my visa expired in a couple of months.

Just before my time was up, I went to Brindavan to see Maharaj-ji. He wasn't seeing the Westerners at all during this period. Apparently, the local visa officials were causing a lot of trouble for the temple because of the Westerners. The officials were asking for bribes, and Maharaj-ji had kicked them out of the temple. Because of this, he wouldn't give us darshan or let us into the back part of the temple where he stayed. The front part of the temple was open to the public, so we'd stand behind the Hanuman temple and watch him over the wall for hours at a time.

I was beginning to panic about not being able to see him before leaving. There were only two days left on my visa, and I had to leave for Delhi later that day to catch a plane and fly to America. As we watched Maharaj-ji sitting outside in the back, one of the other Westerners began to sing *Jaya Jagadish Hare,* a hymn known as *arati* (or waving of lights) that honors the guru. We'd often sung it to him while waving a ghee lamp in a gesture of returning the light to its source.

We'd learned this hymn back in our early days with Maharaj-ji, when we were staying in Nainital and going to Kainchi almost every day. We'd seen the Indian devotees do *guru puja* to Maharaj-ji, and we wanted to do it, too. We enlisted the help of K.K., who sang with great devotion, to teach us the hymn for the puja. Every evening after we returned to our hotel from the temple, K.K. would come over, and we'd practice singing the arati. After some time, we knew it fairly well and decided that we'd surprise Maharaj-ji by doing puja to him in the full-on Indian way. We made elaborate plans to bring all of the traditional accoutrements: flowers, fruit, an arati lamp with ghee wicks, red powdered *kum kum* to put on his forehead, and a bowl to collect the liquid from washing his feet with *panch amrit*—a special mixture of milk, honey, yogurt, sugar, and ghee. Needless to say, we were really excited. We also ordered 80 pounds of Hanuman's favorite sweet—laddus, round balls made from chickpea flour and lots of sugar—to be delivered to the temple on Tuesday.

On Monday, the day *before* our grand puja was to take place, we were at the temple as usual, waiting for Maharaj-ji to come out of his room. All of a sudden, he burst through the doors and sat on the takhat. Like a little kid who couldn't wait a moment longer to open his presents on Christmas morning, he said, "Do the arati! Do the arati!"

Of course, we had nothing with us, so all we could do was stand around him and sing *Jaya Jagadish Hare.* The whole time we were singing, he sat motionless with his eyes closed. When we finished, we stood there staring at him as he continued to sit, still and silent. As I looked at him, my mind was filled with wonder: *I never thought I'd know that I was seeing my guru with these eyes.* For the first time, I knew in my deepest heart that he was my guru. Before this, I *thought* that he was my guru, I *felt* that he was my guru, I *said* that he was my guru, but in this moment, I absolutely *knew* that he was my guru. I deeply realized how my life was flowing into him and through him and how completely he'd accepted me as his devotee. To say that the puja we did to him the next day was anticlimactic doesn't begin to describe it.

Now, at the end of my two-and-a-half years in India, my guru-brothers and I stood singing in the front of the temple. He peeked at us over his shoulder and then turned away again. He started moving his head to the song, but then he turned again, giving us the cold shoulder. Finally, as if he couldn't help himself, he turned toward us and motioned for us to come inside. We ran to him! There was laughing and crying and fruit flying in all directions— total chaos.

I sat there thinking, *I'm about to get on a plane to America. What am I going to do there? What am I going to do in America?* I was completely freaked-out. Part of me insisted, *I've got to ask him . . . I've got to ask him to tell me what to do. I mean—what am I going to do in America?* And then the other side of me said, *No! Have faith, you miserable jerk—you should have faith. What's wrong with you? Just go—have faith! I've got to ask, I've got to ask, I've got to . . . what am I going to do? Have faith!* Back and forth went the Ping-Pong game in my mind until I finally blurted out, "Maharaj-ji, how can I serve you in America?"

I didn't really care about how I could serve him in the U.S. I was freaked and worried about what I would do in America, but I couldn't be honest with myself or with him at that moment. Knowing what was actually in my mind, he looked at me and made a face like he'd just bitten into a sour pickle.

"What?! If you ask about service, it's not service. Just do what you want." In his usual cryptic, inscrutable manner, Maharaj-ji was revealing the highest truth. Real selfless service must come from the depths of our hearts, from who we truly are, not because we're following orders or because we think we *should* be doing it because it would be *good* for us. "Do what you want" was Maharaj-ji's great multileveled gift to me: it propelled me on my lifelong journey and gave me the freedom to find out what I really wanted to do. But I didn't know this then.

Wait a minute. Do what I want? How would that be service? Do what I want?

I couldn't believe my ears. I knew what I wanted to do. And I knew that *he* knew what I wanted to do. I'd been celibate the whole time I was in India, almost three years! When I left the U.S. for India in 1970, I'd said to myself, *The hell with relationships. I'm not getting involved with anybody. I'm taking a break.* So for three years, I'd been celibate. *Three years.* From the ages of 23 to 26. Prime time. Nothing for three years. Was I tense? *Me? Tense?* Do the math!

How could doing what I wanted be of service to him? I sat there, stunned. My mind was like a train stopped dead on the tracks. Then after a moment, he looked over at me, smiled sweetly, and asked, "So, how will you serve me?" Then he cracked up laughing. He bopped me on the head. "Go on, go. Don't get married in America. Jao—go."

My mind was completely blank. It was time for me to leave for Delhi to catch the plane back to the States. I bent down and touched his feet for the last time, and when I looked up, he was beaming at me. "So, how will you serve me in America?" he gently repeated.

I felt like I was moving in a dream. I floated across the courtyard and bowed to him one more time from a distance. As I did, I heard the voice of my heart whispering silently in the depths of my being, "I will sing to you in America."

Here I am with Ram Dass and a few other devotees, meditating on the Himalayas in Kausani: Good-bye to dreams of being a sadhu; hello America! *(Courtesy of Rameshwar Das.)*

111

PART II

Bringing It All Back Home

With Ram Dass at Dharma Festival Boston, 1973 *(Courtesy of Surya Green.)*

SEX, DRUGS, AND GRACE

$\mathcal{W}$hen Maharaj-ji said, "Don't get married in America," there were two ways I could have taken it: one was the way he meant it, and the second was the way I selfishly wanted to understand it. I, of course, chose my own interpretation. In India, theoretically, sex goes with marriage. So when he told me not to get married in America, there was no question that he was instructing me to maintain my celibacy. This is how Maharaj-ji was. He'd casually say something that was so important for you to hear, but you had to be listening. I was going back to the candy store, and I really didn't want to hear what he was saying.

I'd been celibate for those years in India because of my issues with love and sex. I wanted to turn it off, but I couldn't. All of that energy was still there. It had to go somewhere, and not knowing what to do with it was driving me insane. Attachment to and identification with the desires based in the body and the emotions are what bind us to feeling separated from other beings. The reason I'd been celibate wasn't because I was finished with sex. It was exactly the opposite. My mind was on fire with sexual desire and had been my whole life, but I'd never been at ease with my sexuality. I'd never been in a relationship with anyone that had been fully satisfying emotionally.

115

Thinking about my first sexual experience, I remember being so nervous and uptight. When it was over, I jumped up and said to the woman, "I'll go and get us some sandwiches at the deli," and I ran out the door. The minute I'd closed the door behind me, I leaned against the wall and thought, *This is what the whole world is going crazy trying to get?* I thought I was having a spiritual realization, but it was really only my neurotic inability to simply enjoy myself posing as wisdom. I got the sandwiches and went back upstairs.

Now I was returning to the West a stronger, more confident person due to my time with Maharaj-ji. I felt that a lot of my neurotic stuff had dropped away, and unconsciously I was anxious to flex my muscles. It had been a long time since I'd touched another body sexually. There was a huge chasm separating me from "objects of lust." It was scary. But after a few months of being back in America, I met somebody and we got together. We were having a good time, and she came to stay with me. She'd just arrived when I got a letter from one of the Western devotees who was with Maharaj-ji in India. He'd been sitting with Maharaj-ji one day when Maharaj-ji looked around and asked, "Where's Krishna Das?"

"You sent him to America."

"Oh . . . what's he doing?"

So my friend, God bless him, said, "He's chanting in America."

"Oh, he's chanting? Ask him to come back. I want to hear him sing."

When I read the letter, I was so happy that I ran around the house a thousand times like in one of those old Buster Keaton movies, screaming, "I'm going back! I'm going back!"

One of the things Maharaj-ji told me before I returned to America was that I should get a yearlong visa for my next trip to India and $1,000 to support myself while I was there. I hadn't had any money the whole time I'd been in India. Most of the Westerners barely had any money, so the ones who did chipped in and created the "Hanuman fund," and if we needed some, we took it. I had applied for the visa and was saving money, *and* my girlfriend had just come to stay with me. There was a part of me that was resisting running right back to him. And we know which part that was.

I wrote to Maharaj-ji, saying, "I'm ready to come, but you'd instructed me to get a year visa and have a thousand dollars. I've applied for the visa, and I'm working and making some money. Should I wait or come now?" Unconsciously, I was buying some time with my girlfriend, figuring that it would take at least a couple of weeks to get a response. It was mid-July when the reply came. It said. "Maharaj-ji says, 'Come in December.'" I had indeed bought some time to enjoy myself and still had my orders to return. Life was great.

Then on September 11, 1973, Maharaj-ji died. I had blown it. *I had completely blown it!* I knew what he'd meant when he told me not to get married in America, and I'd chosen to ignore it. Now I was paying the price. I would never see him again.

He never asked me for *anything*—he never wanted anything, nor did he ever need anything from anyone. But he'd asked me to come back and sing to him, and I'd turned away. I betrayed his love. There was no doubt in my mind that I'd lost the only chance I would ever have to be happy. Being with him was the only thing that had ever worked for me. It was my only connection to that love, and I'd thrown it away.

I ended things with my girlfriend and went back to India with many of the other Westerners for the cremation, which we were too late to attend. So we went up to the hills to spend some time at his temple in Kainchi. On my first morning there, I woke up to a knock at the door of my room. I opened it to find a young girl holding a flower and some fruit. She told me that Siddhi Ma had sent these things for me because that night she'd had her first dream of Maharaj-ji since he'd left his body. In the dream, she'd been sitting with him, and I was there chanting. I was deeply moved. It eased my anguish for a moment, but nothing could help me through what was to come.

Although my girlfriend and I were no longer a couple when I returned to America, we got back together six years later. We then had a daughter and got married. In Maharaj-ji's eyes, past, present, and future are all visible. So in reality, the moment that my girlfriend and I first slept together, we had indeed gotten married, even if it didn't look that way to me at the time. The importance of his casually spoken instruction to me—"Don't get married in America"—revealed itself to me in a brutally painful way after it was too late.

He knew. He knew everything. When he asked me to come back to India, he'd given me a chance to overcome my own innate tendencies or *vasanas* and break out of them. But I couldn't. And so this was the way my life had to go, schlepping through the valley of the shadow of death. From that point on, for more than 11 years, I lived in deep despair. My heart was dying for the love that I'd betrayed. It was almost unbearable. Despite the fact that my life seemed to be okay from the outside, I was unable to appreciate it and caused much unhappiness to myself and others. I was unable to help myself in any way because I truly believed there was no hope of ever being happy again.

When I'd been with Maharaj-ji in Bombay, one day he'd suddenly sat up and out of the blue said to me, "Courage is a very important thing."

Mr. Barman, who was also sitting there, noted, "But Maharaj-ji, God takes care of His devotees."

Maharaj-ji shot a look at him and then looked back at me. With great intensity, he repeated, "Courage is a very important thing."

There have been times in my life that have been so difficult and painful that the only thing I had to hold on to was the memory of him saying that. I had no courage, but simply remembering the way he looked at me that day gave me enough courage to make it through.

In the early '80s, I got addicted to freebase—a smokable, rather than snortable, form of cocaine. During this time, my mother came to visit me in California for a week or so. She slept in the living room, which was directly above my bedroom. After everybody went to sleep, I'd lock myself in a big closet and smoke freebase coke all night long. I didn't know at the time that my mother was an alcoholic and doing the same thing to herself with booze just a few feet above me. I was stunned when she checked into a rehab center a short time later. I was deeply affected, but not enough to stop.

Soon after this, an old friend died of a drug overdose. I was on my way to Canada to see K.C. Tewari, who was visiting from India. Tewari was one of Maharaj-ji's closest old devotees and a great friend to me. K.C. and his wife, whom I called "Ma," had "adopted" me after Maharaj-ji left his body. They made me a member of their family, and treated me as if I was their eldest son. They fed me and soothed my spirit, which was suffering so much in the absence of Maharaj-ji's physical form.

On the way, I stopped to see my father in New York. I slept in the spare room in his apartment and was up all night smoking freebase. I finished what I had and was panicking, searching the rug for anything that looked like a piece of base, smoking pieces of sock lint from the floor, when all of a sudden the friend who had recently overdosed semi-materialized above me in the room. I realized that she had been "getting off" through me and was, in fact, feeding off of my addiction and intensifying it. Furiously I yelled, "Fuck off!" and she disappeared. Even though I was really messed up, I was seriously shaken by this.

The next morning, I got on the plane to Montreal and drove out to where Tewari was staying. I hadn't seen my Indian "father" in a long time and was very anxious to be with him. I went upstairs to the room he was staying in and saw that he was talking to someone. His back was turned to the door. I stopped in my tracks. Something didn't feel right. I actually began to back out of the room when he turned, pointed his finger at me, and said with an intensity I cannot describe, "Promise me that you will stop cocaine. Promise me *now!*" His eyes were like burning coals. I had no choice—I loved him so much that I had to do it.

"Yes, I promise," I told him. And from that moment on, I never touched freebase again. It was all grace. Without the Tewaris, I probably wouldn't be alive today.

Back in 1971, some of the Westerners in our group in India used to smoke hashish. I wasn't that into it, but every once in a while I did have some tokes. One day we were standing around Maharaj-ji's "office" window, and he was talking and joking with us. All of a sudden he turned to me and, with much the same intensity that K.C. would use on me years later, said, "Promise me that you will give up smoking hashish."

I promised him that I would, but then I began to freak inside. I asked, "Maharaj-ji, what happens if I'm at a party when I'm back in America and someone offers me hash—"

He cut me off, "If you can't do a little thing like this, how will you ever find God?" And he slammed the window shutter in my face. Maharaj-ji was completely beyond time. Nothing was hidden from him. He knew the past and the future. I guess that was a dress rehearsal for the real thing.

I stopped taking psychedelic drugs early in the '70s because I realized that if I ceased going up and down so much, the plateau of consciousness would gradually rise. Part of me knew that I needed to clean my heart and stop trying to escape from my problems. I had to learn to be okay with myself as I am. I saw that the blocks of ice in my heart would melt over time, but unless I could see the shadows that were affecting me, they'd be impossible to remove.

Practices like chanting allow me to see more clearly what forces are working beneath the surface. It's important for us all to develop patience with ourselves—we need to stop running after what we hope will be blissful experiences and instead recognize that it's our own stuff that's preventing us from *being* bliss. I'm no longer attracted to the temporary experiences of ecstasy that psychedelics like LSD can give, and I no longer need to obliterate myself with drugs like cocaine. These days, I'm far more interested in removing the things in me that prevent me from living in love all the time.

Four or five months after I stopped doing coke, I was in a very freaky, discombobulated kind of place. I wasn't doing any drugs, but I was really depressed and miserable. I decided to go to India just to get away. It was the fall of 1984, and I arrived in Kainchi just as Durga puja was beginning. For the next nine days, there would be a sacred fire ceremony with mantras and offerings into the fire. It would go on all day, and many devotees would be gathering at the temple for the festival.

When I arrived, I thought, *Now I can go to my room and crash for a week. I don't have to see or talk to anybody.* Instead, to my horror I heard, "Oh, Krishna Das has come! How wonderful! Come, sit with us in the fire ceremony!" They knew me from the old days with Maharaj-ji and knew that he'd made me the *pujari* (priest) of the Durga Temple in 1972. Everyone was thrilled that I'd shown up. I wasn't so thrilled, but there was no way to refuse. They'd asked with so much love, and I didn't want to hurt them.

All day long, I sat next to the devotee who'd sponsored the puja and made offerings into the fire. It was an honor to be included. We chanted *Swaha* (the mantra of offering) together, but my mental mantra was more like, *Damn! I can't take this—Swaha—goddammit, I want to go to sleep—Swaha—my back hurts.* . . . I hadn't sat cross-legged for such a long time, and I ached all over. Smoke and ashes were everywhere. We also had to fast every day until the ceremony was over at the end of the day. I'd literally gone from the frying pan into the fire.

There was a daily two-hour break between the morning and afternoon pujas. At the end of the morning session, everybody would come up to the front of the temple to do arati to Maharaj-ji's takhat, the place he used to sit. We sang the arati hymn, bowed down, and went to take a rest. I stood to the side and watched, feeling totally closed off and disconnected.

One day after the arati, everybody bowed down and went to rest except one very old lady. She'd bowed down and put her head on the takhat, but she didn't get up. She'd gone into samadhi. When I saw this, it was like a spear through my heart. I thought, *These people are living in his presence! Even now! He's real to them!* It was such a shock to my system. This was 11 years after Maharaj-ji had gone. *He's real to these people!* I felt like I'd been hit by a truck. I staggered over to the side of the temple and sat down. I felt even farther away from him than I had before.

Siddhi Ma had been sitting in Maharaj-ji's room. When she saw me through the window, she sent somebody to get me. I thought, *Oh, why don't they just leave me alone and let me die? I can't stand any more.* But I couldn't say no. "Yeah, okay, coming." I got up and walked through the back door, across the courtyard, and into Maharaj-ji's room. As I came to the door, I saw Ma sitting on the floor at the foot of his bed. Nobody else was in the room. As I crossed the threshold, I was struck by a thunderbolt right in the center of my chest. I fell to the ground like a tree that had been hit by lighting. My heart cracked open, and I felt the incredible sweetness of Maharaj-ji's presence. I was crying uncontrollably and couldn't stop. He had come back to me.

In that instant, every moment of my life from the second that I heard he had died until the present moment passed before my eyes like frames of a movie . . . every second of 11 years in the blink of an eye. I saw everything that had happened to me—everything I'd thought and felt and done, all of the pain and suffering—but I saw it from a completely clear, quiet place. When I'd heard that he died, a wall had gone up around my heart, and I wouldn't let myself feel him anymore. I wouldn't let myself feel love anymore. It was a big wall that surrounded me, and it wouldn't let anything in. In the next instant, I saw that every brick in the wall had a word written on it, flashing like a neon sign: *Anger, Guilt, Shame, Greed, Selfishness, Fear.* That was what the wall was made of, and I was stuck behind it, a prisoner. I suddenly knew, *If I just look at this wall, if I pay attention to what this stuff is, it will start to go away. All I have to do is look at it and not pretend it doesn't exist, and it will start to go away.*

Then I saw that the wall meant nothing to Maharaj-ji. He was in the wall, over the wall, everywhere. He had never left me for a second. *I* had left *him!* I wouldn't allow myself to feel him.

I was still lying there on the floor, sobbing, and Siddhi Ma was still sitting there quietly. I kept thinking, *She must think I'm out of my mind.* I tried to stop crying, but I couldn't. It only made it worse. Then somebody came to the window and said that they were waiting for me to begin the afternoon session of the puja. I had no sense that any time had passed; I was in absolute ecstasy. It felt like I was making love with the whole universe in the middle of my chest, and every breath made it a thousand times more intense. I could hardly stand up. Still sobbing, I went back to the swahas and the puja. I was totally out of my mind with bliss. Every cell was dancing. The devotee who was sitting next to me doing the ceremony kept looking over at me and finally asked, "Krishna Das, are you all right?" I couldn't stop crying. Indians aren't big huggers, but he reached over behind me and kind of patted me on the back and asked, "Has someone died?"

Later in the day, another great devotee of Maharaj-ji's named Mrs. Soni saw me walking across the courtyard, crying. She also asked if I was all right. I looked at her and tried to say something, but I couldn't speak. Holding back tears, I barely managed, "Maharaj-ji. . . !" At this, her eyes rolled up all the way back into her head. She stood in front of me shaking like a leaf for about a minute before they rolled back down. She looked at me and said, "Exactly!" and then floated off across the courtyard.

I was in fat city. I walked around the temple, enjoying this ecstasy. When I noticed that the intensity came down a little bit, all I had to do was inhale deeply into my heart and it came back up. It was so great. I thought, *How compassionate is the Lord! Not only does he give the ecstasy, but he gives the method for keeping it. Oh, how sweet life is!* It went on like this for days.

Then one morning I woke up completely dead inside. I felt like an old building that had burned down and been rained on, and then the dogs had come and pissed all over the place. I was frantically taking deep breaths, but nothing was happening. I almost killed myself trying to breathe the ecstasy back. Nothing worked. I completely flipped out and rushed down the path and climbed up to the roof of the building at the back of the temple.

Kainchi is set like a jewel in a valley in the foothills of the Himalayas. There's a running river, lush green mountains, and electric blue sky. And there I was, a crazy Westerner storming back and forth on the roof of this building, screaming at Maharaj-ji at the top of my lungs: "If you're going to close me down, then don't open me up! Just leave me alone!" On and on, for an hour, just screaming at the top of my lungs. I was furious. I couldn't stand it—I wanted that bliss back!

Tewari came up on the roof to talk to me, but I screamed him back down. Finally Siddhi Ma sent someone to get me, "Siddhi Ma calling!" *Good! Because I'm going home, and I'm going to tell her.* She was sitting in the Tewaris' room, and I walked up to the doorway and stood there glaring. She glanced up at me and said something in Hindi. Everybody in the room giggled. In a deep, angry voice, I asked, "What did she say?" I was told that she'd observed I was like a little kid who'd been given a candy and gobbled it up in one bite and wanted another one right away. I couldn't have another one right away, but I shouldn't worry, I'd have another candy someday.

It was like Maxwell's silver hammer coming down on my head. I was immediately brought back to Earth. I muttered, "Oh. Okay. I . . . I'm going to go lie down now, okay? Yeah. I . . . I'm just going to go to my room, okay?" I slept for about 24 hours, and when I woke up, I was back to normal. Except everything had changed. I'd been given another chance. It was as if they said, "All right, let the kid live." *Bam!* From that moment on, I *knew* that it was okay to be alive. I hadn't blown it. I would be okay. It was okay to go through my nonsense. It was the beginning of another chapter of my life. I hadn't blown it—*I hadn't blown it!* Grace.

That's when I came back to the States and got into therapy.

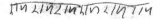

MAHARAJ-JI—"EVERYTHING WILL BE ALL RIGHT."

[Photo courtesy of Balaram Das]

SRI HANUMAN, BRINDAVAN, 1972.

[Photo courtesy of Roy Bonney]

MAHARAJ-JI ON THE WALL OF KAINCHI TEMPLE.

[PHOTO COURTESY OF BALARAM DAS]

MAHARAJ-JI—LOST IN LOVE.

[Photo courtesy of Balaram Das]

KAINCHI VALLEY.

[PHOTO COURTESY OF ROY BONNEY]

NAINITAL HIGH, 1971.

[Photo courtesy of Mohan Baba]

KRISHNA DAS ON THE YAMUNA, 1971.

[PHOTO COURTESY OF RAMESHWAR DAS]

SRI SIDDHI MA.

[Photo courtesy of Rameshwar Das]

Movie of Me

The love that I felt coming from Maharaj-ji when I was with him in India was so extraordinary and unusual because it kept flowing. It didn't come to me if I was good, and it didn't stop flowing to me if I was bad . . . and he knew everything. There was no way that I deserved this love. Of course, that's the nature of grace; no one *deserves* it. That's why they call it grace. It comes to us when we least expect it—when we are at the end of our rope and can't see how we can go on anymore, we turn a corner and there it is. We trip and fall and we're in it. Grace surrounds us all the time, but we only feel it at rare moments. It is the true state of the Universe. As Suzuki Roshi said, "Come walk with me in the rain. But don't hurry. It's raining everywhere."

What keeps us away from the gentle rain of grace? It's our endless obsession, all day long, with *I, me, mine.* We wake up in the morning and start writing "the movie of Me": *What am I going to do? Where am I going to go? How am I going to get there? Is this enough? Is it too much? What's going to happen? What am I going to wear? How do I look? Does he like me? Why not?* All day long. The movie of Me. We write it, direct it, produce it, and star in it. We write reviews that we read and get depressed! Then we go to sleep and do it again the next day. I've seen it so many times. And still, every time I turn on the TV, there it is: me, myself, and my stuff.

Gradually (key word) and inevitably (the other key word), spiritual practices like chanting remove this subjective version of life by slowly dissolving the attachments that keep us feeling separate from the people around us, and separate and cut off from the beauty that lives in our own hearts. Everything we do in life is connected to everyone and everything else, but because we're locked up in our own little world, when we reach out to touch another person, all we touch is our version of the other person, and all they touch is their version of us. We're rarely *really* touching each other.

In 1997, when I first started traveling around to chant with people, a friend of mine arranged for me to lead kirtan in Tucson, Arizona, at a Middle-Eastern restaurant called The Caravan. I was going to be singing in a small waiting area that was part of the entrance to the restaurant. On the other side of this room was the kitchen. I was sitting on the floor with my friend Bub, who was drumming; the eight or nine people who showed up to sing were sitting in chairs by the walkway that the customers and the waitpersons took to get to the dining room.

Customers were staring at us quizzically; food was going back and forth from the kitchen; pots and pans were being washed; espresso was being made; and there I was, singing and thinking, *This is as bad as it gets!* But I was wrong. As I was about to start singing the last chant of the night, *Namah Shivaya*, two big Native American guys—they had to be over six feet tall and 300 pounds each—wandered into the restaurant radiating an aura of alcohol. They plopped down in the two empty chairs right in front of me and stared blankly. I thought, *I'm going to sing my ass off because I will probably be dead before the chant is over.*

I started singing. And I really sang. When Bub and I finished, we ended with a long *Om.* Then it was quiet except for the noise from the kitchen. I was sitting with my eyes closed when I realized that one of the guys had gotten up and was standing over me, staring down. I looked up at this mountain of a man. *Now what, Maharaj-ji? What are you going to do to me now?* The man said, "I'm Native American. [Pause.] I was in Vietnam. [Pause.] I know the real thing when I hear it. [Looong pause.] And you got it." As he wandered away, I started to breathe again.

I'd been so caught up in the movie of Me—my own program of who and what I was afraid of—that there had been no room to see who this person really was. It was very humbling to recognize how deeply I was caught in my own projections, even after a whole night of chanting.

All of us live in our own universe to some extent. We must become aware of the way these programs of ours work, and how they color our lives and cut us off from other people, seeing them only from far behind our private barricades. Everybody brings their own past and carries their own future within them at every moment. We carry the sense that we are the most important thing in the universe and everybody else exists in relation to us. I look at you and see the way you dress and your hair, and it brings up a lot of unconscious assumptions about who you are. It's not who you are; it's only my version of you. This is what human beings do. Buddha said that comparing is actually the last kind of thinking to go. We're always comparing: *She's higher than me. He's this. She's that.* All day long, we see ourselves through the eyes of other people.

िन्त्म ८/न्2 िन्त्न ८/न 7/न

On one of my visits to Kainchi after Maharaj-ji left his body, I was sitting on the roof with one of the kirtan walas, a young Bengali drummer, and he was asking me about my life. He asked me if I was married, which I was at the time. I said, "Yeah," thinking about the difficulties in that relationship. He sighed wistfully. Then he asked, "You have kids?"

And again I said, "Yeah," thinking about all of the stuff they'd have to go through.

"Oooh. Do you have a home?"

"Yeah." This time, I was actually thinking about the mortgage payments.

"Wow. You got a car?"

"Two."

"Wow!"

He wanted everything I had.

I looked at him and said, "Hey! What's wrong with you? Are you crazy?! What do you want all of these problems for? All you have to do is wake up in the morning, do some chanting, and go to sleep! That's the whole thing: you get fed, you get a place to sleep. What's your problem?"

He thought I was crazy; I thought he was crazy. It was an interesting moment, especially in light of the fact that these days all *I* do is wake up in the morning, do some chanting, and go to sleep!

One time Maharaj-ji was sitting with some of his devotees, and he started saying, *"Tul tul, nan nan, tul tul, nan nan,"* which means, "Too much, too much, too little, too little, too much, too much, too little, too little." And he went on like this for more than an hour, just sitting there: "Too much, too much, too little, too little, too much, too much, too little, too little . . ."

Somebody asked, "Maharaj-ji, what are you saying?"

"This is your minds! This is what you people *do* all the time."

As someone who's very much bound by his own likes and dislikes, as soon as anything happens, my judgmental mind instantly arises. I immediately think that I know whether it's good or bad for me and whether I like it or don't like it. Tewari used to say that the judgmental mind—analyzing things from our own limited point of view—is like being in a boat going down the rapids toward a waterfall and looking at the bank and thinking that the bank is moving. We think we're seeing everything clearly, but we're headed for the waterfall. Tewari had a totally nonjudgmental way of seeing the world and of living in the world, and often showed me what it might look like if I wasn't caught in the movie of Me.

Spiritual practices can slow down the movie of Me. Gradually, we negotiate a truce with what we perceive as the so-called world outside of us. The immediacy of our knee-jerk reactions slows down and we get a chance to *not* react so quickly. We make a deal with ourselves not to believe everything we think, to allow ourselves some time to go by so that we can see if our reactions are based on what's really happening or what we think is happening. We move in the direction of that less reactive inner place where ✳ we feel better about ourselves because there's more peace. That's where the love is hidden. This tentative truce is like foreplay. We approach the Beloved that lives within us—the same Beloved that lives within every being—and we begin to experience what it really means to live in love. Whenever we do any practice, read a holy book, or do anything that opens us up, we're going against the grain of all that unconscious, automatic moviemaking.

When we start to do a practice like chanting, we don't really believe it's going to work. We kind of *hope* it's going to be good for us, but we can't imagine what the result of a practice will be, and that's the point. If we could imagine it, it would simply be another projection of our own minds and not something that arises from deep within us. We know we're looking for something, and we know we don't feel the way we want to, but we don't know *how* we'll feel when we begin to feel the way we hope to feel. When this presence within us—our own true nature, who we really are, the One, the Self, God, Guru, Buddha Nature—begins to arise, ✳ something happens for which we're not really prepared: we begin to get happy. Then our whole day is ruined. Since we spend all of our time trying to get happy or get rid of the things that make us unhappy, what do we do with our lives when we wake up happy?! May all beings have this problem.

If we're attracted to chanting, it's because something we hear in the chanting or the way the chanting affects us feels right. We want more of that feeling. When I walked into the room in New Hampshire with Ram Dass for the first time, I had that feeling of rightness, of *Yes! This is real.* I knew this feeling, but I'd never tasted it like that before. Nor did I know at the time how to find it for myself. Many years went by before I could trust myself enough to find my way more deeply into that place. But once any of us touch that place, we begin to look for it again and again, in everything we do in life. We find things that help us *stay* in that place. We try *anything,* like I did—drugs, sex, rock 'n' roll—but nothing worked well enough and long enough. I was finally forced to look within.

Our own longing forces us to find what works in our lives to bring us to that place, and to let go of the things that keep us out of that place. It's all in *here,* not out there. But we've been so programmed not to trust, or even to be aware of our feelings and our intuition about things, that it's very difficult. Also, it's not that easy to maintain. We have to keep pulling the plug on the inner programs that prevent us from feeling the way we know it's possible to feel. Practice helps us find and remove the plug.

The way things look to us at night is very different from the way they look in the daylight. We know and accept this simply and naturally. When the sun begins to rise and the sky starts to get light, the things that surround us begin to take on a more distinct shape. We also move and act differently according to how clearly we can see. When the golden sun of that loving presence begins to rise in our hearts, our lives start to look very different. Confusion falls away. The fear of the dark and what's hidden there begin to disappear. We start to relax; we feel differently about ourselves and others. As we see and feel, so do we act. No one has to tell us anything, because we learn from the inside that all good things appear on their own in our lives as the sun of love rises.

Chanting ends the enchantment of the movie of Me by calling out/calling in to that love. As it fills us with light and presence, it brings freedom from our own subjective way of seeing things, our own version of life. Ultimately, we're lifted into the bright sky of the heart where we see very clearly that we're all a part of the great One. We're all inside this radiant Being, this vast presence. Nothing is outside of that. We have found our heart of gold at last.

Siddhi Ma sitting with Maharaj-ji. *(Courtesy of Shrish Jagati.)*

RELATIONSHIPS

ललित राम

When Maharaj-ji looked at the other devotees and me, we felt complete and total acceptance. We felt loved so intimately that it was scary sometimes. It wasn't something I'd ever tasted before. Where I came from, love was conditional: "If you're cool to me, I'll be cool to you. I won't love you anymore if you don't . . ." That's not what it was about with him. He knew who we really were. He knew what we'd done in our lives, and it didn't affect his love. He could see right through our personalities, right to God inside of us, right to our own true Being. And the power of his seeing allowed us to let go of our stuff and enter into that love.

The second he looked away, I crashed. Then he'd look back and go, "Hee hee hee." It's terrible to be such a fool. A fool for love. I couldn't protect myself against that because it was everything I ever wanted. My wildest desire of how it was going to feel when it was *exactly the way I wanted it to be* is the way it was sitting with him. Forget about being cool, I just ran for it. But what was really scary was to see how I closed down every ten seconds. There I was, sitting with this guy who was loving me beyond belief, and I couldn't hold on to it. I tried, *believe me,* I tried.

If you've ever seen hummingbirds at the sugar drip, you know they don't go too far away while there's sugar available. Similarly, let's say that you went to a party and met that perfect someone. You're thinking, *Wow!* Then somebody introduces the two of you and you have a little conversation, and that person's looking at *you* like you're looking at *her*. *Double wow!* You get up the courage to ask for her phone number—and she *gives* it to you! "Oh thanks, yeah . . . I'll call you . . . okay, sure." You go home that night, but you can't sleep much. You wake up at six in the morning, but it's too early to call. So you wait. Finally, it's the appropriately cool hour to call—not too early, not too late. You call and she says, "Oh wow, I was just thinking of you. You want to come over?"

"Oh yeah, sure!" Are you going to *walk* across town? No way. You're going to rent a helicopter to drop you at her house. Why? Because you know she (or he or *it*) is there waiting.

It's all here waiting for us inside, but we got the phone number wrong. So we're dialing every number, every combination of those numbers, trying to get it right. One day we'll say the Name right *once, wholeheartedly,* and the connection will be completed. Chanting the Name takes away those thoughts that tell us, *Ah, it'll never happen. I can't do this. I don't deserve this love. I'm not enough. I'm not tall enough. My hair's not curly enough.* Whatever. All of the stories we tell ourselves that turn us off—that's what we can let go of through doing practice. And what's left is what's already always here.

Lama Surya Das has said, "Enlightenment is an accident. We spend our whole lives trying to be more accident-prone." We long for these accidental moments of love. At such moments, finding ourselves in that love, we see ourselves as beautiful through the eyes of love. Of course, the whole point is that it's possible to feel that way always. When we develop the eyes of love, then we see everything and everyone, including ourselves, the way Maharaj-ji saw us.

It's easy to imagine what it's like when we love somebody else. When we're in love, when we feel loved, we go through the day in a different way. It's simple. Lightning doesn't shoot through the sky; we just start to feel better regardless of what's happening. But what if that *somebody* we love is *us?* How would that feel? It's very difficult to imagine, isn't it? We see ourselves so harshly and judge ourselves so incessantly about everything. Practice is a time when we're specifically dedicated to letting go of those kinds of patterns.

During one of Joseph Goldstein's *metta* (lovingkindness) meditation retreats, a man who was having difficulty offering himself lovingkindness said, "I want to be the guy my dog thinks I am." Can you imagine if that's who we thought we were? It would be amazing!

We're in relationship to everything, all the time. It seems that the bottom line with relationships is this: As much as you love yourself, that's as much as you will be able to love another and allow yourself to be loved. Most of the Indian people I've met don't have the same issues with this. Love was not withheld from them as children, so as adults they're easier with intimacy and love. They don't expect the other person to save them from themselves, their loneliness, their lack of self-love—all of the stuff that we in the West do.

In every relationship I was in, I kept trying to find Maharaj-ji —my source, my touchstone for the feeling of love I so wanted. Needless to say, this put a bit of a burden on relationships with other people. One day I was with a friend of mine who's very psychic and we were talking about relationships. She said, "You know, you already have the main relationship of your life with Maharaj-ji. Why do you keep trying to re-create it and find it in other people?" When she said that, I saw that Maharaj-ji was the great jewel and that all of my other relationships—romantic, nonromantic, whatever—are smaller jewels set around the one great jewel. If I didn't try to make them into the big stone, they were cool just the way they were. That was a big revelation for me.

We want to connect with people, to be in relationship, and to have community. We want to have a partner and be able to enjoy that. When we get intense with other human beings, then we have an opportunity to see all of our stuff. In fact, we can't miss it! Most of us forget that sex and love are two different things and experience great disappointment when love doesn't show up with sex.

Once I was telling Tewari about my girlfriend. I was going on and on about how much I loved her. Finally when I was done, he smiled at me and said, "My boy, relationships are a business. Do your business! Enjoy yourself—there's no harm! But love is what is always here; it's what lasts the whole 24 hours."

Tewari, who was happily married with a large family, was giving me the bottom line again: Love is what we *are;* we don't get it from somebody, we can't give it to anybody, we can't fall in it or fall out of it. Love is our true Being. He was pointing out that I was still looking for the "perfect" relationship, the "perfect" love with another human being. I was imagining that when I "found" it, I'd be completely happy forever. I got so angry at him that I didn't talk to him for days.

But, of course, he was right.

He was saying that love is not something we "get" from people; it's always here, yet we can't find it because we're looking outside ourselves. He was saying that our relationships with other people, based as they are on the mistaken belief that we're separate from each other, are really a "business." In a sense, we're doing business—bartering our affection and attention in order to attract another person who will do the same for us.

Tewari wasn't saying that this was "bad" in any way. He told me to enjoy it, that there was nothing wrong with satisfying my emotional and physical desires. He was simply pointing out that water can't come from a stone, and if I expected a relationship to make me happy forever, I was going to be very disappointed. When we eat a bowl of pasta, we don't expect that it will satisfy our hunger forever and that we'll never need to eat another bowl of pasta again. Why do we think that a relationship will do that? Why, when we fall in love, do we think, *This is forever?* Well, that's why they call it "falling."

We can share attention, caring, and affection with another person, but real love is within us. It's the same in everyone . . . it's the nature of the soul, of our very being.

> *The emotion that overpowers you for a minute*
> *and passes away the next instant,*
> *that cannot be called love.*
> *That is Love which ever remains kindled*
> *and enlivened in this body all the twenty-four hours.*
> *Everyone takes the Name of Love but*
> *none truly recognises its essence.*
> *That which endures all the twenty-four hours,*
> *that is Love.*

— Kabir[14]

I was once at a teaching with a Tibetan lama who asked, "Why do Westerners think that relationships are supposed to make you happy?" He couldn't believe it!

In relationships, we're navigating through our world, and other people are navigating through theirs. When they do or say something that we react to, we rarely ask ourselves (or them) what they really mean. Usually, we take for granted that our version of the story—our reaction to what we think they did or said, which we see through the filter of our movie of Me—is perfectly reasonable. We don't question it at all. We accept what we've seen through our own lens. For instance, *She doesn't like me. She thinks I'm a schmuck.* But do we have any proof that this is what the other person is actually thinking? Ninety-nine percent of the time, other people have no idea that their words or actions triggered such a reaction in us, and they're confused and hurt by their perception of our reaction. We're both lost in our programs. This is very much the state of our daily lives. We're swimming around in the sea, bumping up against each other, and rarely questioning whether or not our reactions are based on what really happened or our own subjective version of it.

Our lives are full of unconsciously accepted beliefs about the way things are. When I was younger, my mother was often angry, judgmental, and hard to please. Now I'll find myself in a relationship with a woman and often unconsciously assume that she's judgmental of me and hard to please. I'll interpret a lot of stuff through that old lens, making knee-jerk assumptions about what that person is thinking about me when I don't really have a clue. Once, for example, at the beginning of one of my relationships, I was so uptight and nervous when we had our first kiss that I thought, *This is really terrible. She must think I'm a jerk.* I got really depressed. Luckily we talked about it later, and she said that it was the greatest kiss she had ever experienced! All of a sudden hell turned to heaven.

Let's say that I've just been shot into outer space by one of these big knee-jerk reactions. Say I had the perception, *Oh, she turned away,* which I immediately turned into *I'm unlovable and useless,* which then turned into anger at being rejected and caused me to respond in a defensive way, to which the other person responded accordingly. We might have a fight on our hands, with neither one of us knowing where it came from.

We all have to learn to apply the strength we get from practice to becoming more aware of how these unconscious programs color our lives. These days, I find myself able to ask myself, *Wait a minute, what if that didn't actually happen? What if that person's facial expression didn't mean "fuck off"? What if they just had a headache?*

I once met Roshi Philip Kapleau, the author of *The Three Pillars of Zen.* He was one of the first Westerners to go to Japan and do intense practice there. He was suffering from very advanced Parkinson's disease and had terrible physical discomfort, along with the involuntary spasms that come from the disease. One thing he said to me really stuck. As he was sitting there, writhing, he looked into my eyes and said with great intensity, "It doesn't matter how much practice you do. If you don't bring it into your daily life, it is all a waste." The power of this statement came from the depths of his realization and his daily battle with Parkinson's, and it shot straight into my heart.

We don't want to walk around afraid. We don't want to walk around feeling hurt and separate. We don't want to continue carrying around all of the feelings of betrayal and pain that we've experienced in all of the relationships of our lives. No matter how much meditation, chanting, yoga poses, or any other practice we do, it's very hard to remove the fears that come up in our daily lives and the feeling of being isolated from the rest of the world. But the result of a true spiritual practice ultimately must be the lessening of that fear and isolation. We can't be judging ourselves if we're really singing or offering ourselves or someone else lovingkindness. These are the moments we're taking energy away from unconscious programs that run all the time in our heads about how small we are or how unworthy we are of love and affection.

We have a lot to worry about in our daily lives, a lot of stress. We move very fast and often get lost in the unconscious flow of our days. We can't control the things outside of us. We can't make people act the way we want them to act. We can't even make *ourselves* act the way we want to act! The good news is that our feeling of unworthiness, our self-judgment, is just *stuff;* it's not who we are. Stuff comes and stuff goes. What doesn't come and go is *who* we really are and *what* we really are. To experience this, we need a spiritual practice.

When we are doing a practice and begin to experience lighter states of being, we start to recognize that being greedy, fearful, jealous, angry, pushy, and manipulative in our relationships actually *hurts*. When we're stuck in one of those heavy states— which for most of us is all we've known—who suffers more than we do? Nobody. We may feel righteous about our heaviness and think that somebody else caused our suffering, but we're the ones who are burning! At these moments it's very hard to practice. For example, if I'm really upset about something, it's very hard to sit down and chant. Sometimes I have to burn for a while until I can begin to let go and return to my practice.

Once I was taking my daughter, Janaki, back to her mother's house, from whom I'd been separated for about two years at this point. My daughter and I were talking about the difficulties of separation. As we pulled into the driveway, I sighed and said, "Relationships are very hard work, you know?"

Janaki looked at me and said, "No! How am I supposed to know that? I'm ten!"

Aaah.

MOTHER PUJA

$\overline{\mathcal{T}\mathcal{D}} \mathcal{L}/\mathcal{D}$

Sometimes when people in a relationship would be having a problem, they'd talk to Maharaj-ji about it. One couple told him, "We're fighting all the time."

Maharaj-ji looked at the man and with great sincerity said, "Just see her as your mother."

Incredulous, the guy replied, "I *hate* my mother!"

Maharaj-ji was amazed and kept asking, "What did he say? What did he say?"

The great saint Shakaracharya wrote a hymn in praise of the Goddess called "May the Goddess Forgive Us." In it, there is a line that's repeated over and over: "A bad son may be born in this world, but never a bad mother." Being born in the West, we're taught that we're born, we live for a while, and then we die—and there is nothing other than this, no other context or understanding of life. For us, life is primarily about feeding ourselves and the few people we're responsible for; that is, getting the most we can and that's that. "The one with the most toys wins."

We have no idea what life is and what it means to be alive. We have no appreciation of what it means to have a human body and what is truly possible in life. Instead, we see life as an ongoing struggle with no happy ending in sight. Because of this, we don't respect and treasure the gift of life that we've gotten from our parents, especially the one who gave birth to us.

In India, they can't conceive of hating one's mother. They have an entirely different emotional shape over there. There is a love among family members—not only among immediate family members, but also among the extended family—that's sorely missing in many Western families. I remember attending the wedding of the Tewaris' eldest grandson in India, where all of the cousins and aunts and uncles were gathered together for the celebration. On the way back from the first ceremony, the family stopped at Kainchi to get Sri Siddhi Ma's blessings. I was sitting with them and marveling at all the love among the family members. I got very emotional, and Ma turned to me. "See? This is what you missed by being born in America," she pointed out. It was shockingly true.

A few days earlier, I'd asked her why Westerners have so much trouble accepting love and feeling loved. She said, "It's because of samskaras [the influence created by our karma]; they can be helpful or obstructing. The food your parents ate, what they were thinking, and the food *you* ate all affect this. Also, parents may withhold affection from children if the children don't behave as they want them to." This teaches little girls and boys that love can be taken away and can be used against them. She implied that it was different in Indian families.

When I lived with the Tewaris, I was shocked to find a functional family. I didn't know that such a thing existed! They argued and fought and carried on, but there was never the slightest feeling that love would or could be lost or withheld. No one in the family had any fear that another would throw them out of his or her heart. It was a wonderful experience for me. K.C. and I would often argue intensely, yelling at each other and getting angry . . . and we were arguing about spiritual things! He'd say something that he knew would piss me off and then bait me with, "You will fire upon me now?" He loved it, and so did I. It was an incredible feeling to be nose to nose, eye to eye, screaming and looking into each other's eyes with total love and joy.

When I was growing up, no one in my house raised their voice, but the atmosphere was filled with the threat of emotional violence. I learned early on that in order to get from the garage, through the door, into the kitchen, and up the stairs to my bedroom (where I could close and lock my door), I needed to be fully armed and on guard—ready to defend myself at any moment. To survive living with my mother, I had to have a secret life inside my room, behind the locked door. I had no other safe place to be myself. This pattern then kept resurfacing in my relationships: I'd unconsciously pick a partner from whom I'd have to protect and hide myself, re-creating my childhood emotional landscape.

My parents were good people, and the last thing either of them wanted to do was hurt my sister or me. But because they didn't love and accept themselves, how could they teach us to do that? My mother was angry at her life. She could not allow herself to be loved, and had no choice but to transmit that mind-set to me. But we always kept in touch no matter where I was in the world. "How you doin'?" "Okay." "What's happening?" "This and that." There was caring and contact, but my mother had countless ways to deflect my love. And when she couldn't deflect it, she drop-kicked me into the next universe. I knew my maternal grandparents, so I came to understand that she didn't have the tools to act in any other way. She was simply carrying on the family tradition.

I'd been in India for two years and was recovering from hepatitis when one day Maharaj-ji looked at me and asked, "Is your mother coming to India?"

"What?" I replied in confusion. "My mother? Coming to India? I don't think so . . ."

The next day, I got a message at the hotel that my mother had called and said she wanted to come to India!

I immediately called her back. "Hi Ma, how are you doing?"

"I want to come see you."

"Uh, okay, but I have to ask Maharaj-ji."

"What?!"

Can you imagine telling your mother that she can't come see you unless your guru says it's okay? But that's what I did. I was petrified to have her come, telling her that I'd call her back the next day. When I went to the temple, I let Maharaj-ji know that my mother wanted to come for a visit.

He said, "Oh, really?"

"Yeah. Can she come?"

"Yes. Tell her to come."

I later found out that she'd told my sister, "I'm going to bring your brother back." Thankfully, it didn't work out that way, at least at that time.

Maharaj-ji was very loving to my mother. I'd asked her to bring him the best sweater she could find, and she brought a beautiful maroon turtleneck from the U.S. He made such a big deal about it. He'd tease the Indian devotees, saying, "You people don't care anything about me. You come here for your own purposes. Look at this woman. She came from so far away and carried this sweater for me." He wore it for a long time. He gave her the name Yasoda, who was Krishna's foster mother. He also gave her flowers to take to Jesus' tomb in Jerusalem, which she planned to visit on her way back to America.

There's a picture of her taken on the lake in Nainital, where we stayed. She's sitting in a boat and looks so beautiful in that moment, so at peace . . . a completely different person than she was at home.

Before she left India, I took my mother to the plains to see the Taj Mahal and do some touring. As we left Kainchi to go on our trip, we walked out of the temple and crossed the bridge over the river. We were about to get into the car and drive away when Mom looked back down into the temple where Maharaj-ji was sitting. All of a sudden, she burst out crying like a baby. Up to the day she died she had no idea what happened in that moment. She had much suffering in her life, but whenever anyone asked her about her visit to India, a strange look would come over her face and she'd tell her story like a child, full of wonder. But then when it was over, she'd go back to her usual self.

The entire three weeks she was in India, I led her around, fed her, and took care of her. Before I finally put her back on the plane to the West, Maharaj-ji told me, "When you take her to Delhi, do puja to her—worship her as the Divine Mother, as the Goddess. You have to bow down to her in the airport."

My mother and me [sitting, right] with Maharaj-ji, 1972. *(Courtesy of S. Kagel.)*

As per Maharaj-ji's instructions, here I am on my knees, worshipping my mother in the Delhi airport. *(Courtesy of S. Kagel.)*

Mom was diagnosed with lung cancer in 1997, but because of early detection, she was declared completely free of it after the operation. Six years later, however, a new cancer developed. By the time she was diagnosed, she only had a few weeks to live. I was with her pretty much 24/7 for those last days of her life. I slept in the guest room of her apartment. The walls were very thin, and at night the sound of the radio in her room would wake me up. I discovered that she'd be awake most of the night, listening to programs about financial planning. It hurt to see how much she was still consumed by her fears and worries about money and life in general. She had no way to let go, no way to calm her mind. The importance of spiritual practice was brought home to me very powerfully as I watched her struggle.

I was very grateful for the opportunity to help my mother. In fact, I realized that I'd waited my whole life for a chance to do something for her. She'd always kept me at a distance, but now that she was so ill, she was too weak to push me away. And sometimes it seemed as if she didn't even want to. She was sick and I was there, and she was letting herself enjoy our time together. We got very close at the end. She told me that I was the best nurse she ever had. When she was shifted to the hospital, I'd sit with her late into the night, being with her in a deep, sweet flow of love.

But she was still my mom! One time she asked for a drink of water and, as I leaned over her, I knocked against the tray on her lap. She snapped at me ferociously, and I recoiled as if I'd been hit in the stomach. As I stood back up, I had an epiphany: from the time I was a small child, even before I could remember, she must have been doing this to me in just the same way. The fact that I couldn't remember it was a shock to my system. I realized that I couldn't remember it because I'd taken shape as a person in reaction to the way she'd treated me. My emotional shape was so deeply formed that *it* couldn't see *itself!* Nonetheless, it still had to be functioning under the surface. I was stunned and amazed.

During my mother's last days, the love between us surfaced when she came out of her sedation and we got a chance to really be with each other. I felt as if we truly met, and that both of us loved and forgave each other fully.

When Mom finally passed, I had another extraordinary realization. I saw that she'd been like a huge electromagnet, and I was held in an emotional shape in much the same way as iron filings take the shape of the magnetic field around a magnet. With her death, the plug on that magnet was pulled, and my iron filings relaxed into a more natural shape for me. The force that had been pulling and shaping me since I was a baby was gone; I felt as if I'd been given much more comfortable clothes to wear, clothes that fit *me* as I am. I was free to be myself and breathe in a new and different way. My mother was also free to go on to new things. We had freed each other with love and were no longer chained together by our emotional programming. It was a very liberating experience, and so totally unexpected that it took many months for me to understand what had happened.

Each generation programs the next one. So much of what we believe about ourselves comes from what our parents believe about themselves, which in turn came from their parents. A friend of mine once told me, "You were parented harshly, so you parent yourself harshly." It was a revelation for me. I left home when I was 18, but I brought my parents with me and would not give myself a break. I lived my life protecting myself against the darkness and unhappiness that I expected to come at any moment.

We take what we've learned from our mothers and fathers—yet when we have our own children, we're horrified to see ourselves repeat our parents' behavior or hear their words and their tone of voice coming from our mouths. Fortunately, the chain can be broken.

I was once really upset about something, and when I came into the house, my daughter, Janaki, was sitting in the kitchen. As I stormed through, I noticed that she hadn't cleaned up the dishes, and I snapped at her the way my mother would have snapped at me. I'll never forget the way she looked at me. She was astounded that I was in such a weird space. She didn't take it personally at all. She just looked at me like I was from some other planet. And because she didn't take it in, by the time I'd finished walking through the kitchen, I saw how stupid I was acting and dropped the whole thing. She'd wisely rejected the legacy and freed me from it, too.

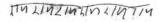

METTA: THE PRACTICE
OF LOVINGKINDNESS

It's all about love. We fall in love with ourselves the minute we see *our true Being.* There's no other option. It's so beautiful. If we really believed that we were worthy of love—and that, in fact, we *are* the love that's waiting for us within our own hearts— every second of our day would be different. Every single second. Immediately.

At one point in my life, I was doing a lot of sitting meditation. Every day I'd go into my little closet, light some incense, and sit down on my fancy meditation cushion. One day I lit the incense, but before my ass hit the cushion, I saw the whole thing clearly. I saw that I was meditating to create a "me" I could like because I didn't like myself the way I was. So my motivation was essentially self-hatred. What good can come from acting out of negative motivations like anger, fear, greed, or shame? This is how neuroses can co-opt spiritual practice. It would have been good if I'd kept sitting after seeing through this false motivation, but my self-loathing was so intense at the time that I got angry with myself and didn't continue meditating.

One way to counteract negative emotions and create a more relaxed inner environment is to introduce what are called "wholesome thoughts." The practice of offering *metta*, the Pali word for "lovingkindness," helps us short-circuit our automatic judgmental reactions about ourselves and other people that are based on our old unconscious programming. Through the practice of metta, we cultivate the ability to wish ourselves and other people well, regardless of who we think they are.

The practice of metta was first given by Buddha to some of his monks. He sent them to meditate in the forest, but when they got there, the local tree demons kept disturbing their practice. They returned to the Buddha and asked for some weapon to deal with these troublesome spirits. The Buddha said that he'd give them the most powerful weapon in the world, and he proceeded to teach them the lovingkindness practice. The story goes that those nasty spirits became transformed into protectors of the dharma.

One of the results of this practice is that we actually begin to see people from a less reactive place, and our judgmental programming is replaced by caring and lovingkindness. As time goes on, we start to get used to living like that, so we plant fewer seeds that will grow into negative states of mind. To put it simply, we become happier.

Sharon Salzberg, the co-founder of Insight Meditation Society, teaches the metta practice. Some years ago, she gave the opening speech at the *Yoga Journal* conference, and there was a line of people around the block wanting to meet her afterward. Why? Because she gave these men and women the permission and space to acknowledge their own suffering and unhappiness. In her talk she showed that there was no reason to try to hide it; it was actually part of the human condition. It was definitely nothing to be ashamed of, and it could be dealt with.

For the most part, the way Westerners approach the spiritual path doesn't include psychological and emotional issues. The emphasis is on the physical. There's no sense trying to erect an outer shell of perfection and flawlessness when we're hurting inside. So when Sharon said that it was okay to admit this, people were drawn to connect with her.

When I took my first metta meditation course with her, I was surprised that I wasn't asked to sit and fight with my mind. Instead, I was to sit and repeat a version of these four phrases:

> *May I be safe*
> *May I be happy*
> *May I be healthy*
> *May I live at ease of heart*

Piece of cake, I thought. I had no idea what I was in for! I began to repeat the phrases and, as instructed, tried to feel some connection with them, not just mindlessly repeat them. "May I be safe. May I be happy. May I be healthy. May I live at ease of heart. May I be safe . . ." I was feeling nothing. Dead meat! I realized that I was totally incapable of wishing myself well at all! It was quite a shock, and I went into a whole mental meltdown as the day progressed. I wondered what was wrong with me and how I could be so psychologically damaged. I thought, *This is never gonna work!* But I kept going.

Then on the second day, we were asked to offer the phrases to someone who'd always been on our side, someone we could always go to for love and support. I picked someone in my life who fit that description and started offering the phrases to that person. In no time at all I began to feel light and free and full of joy. This wonderful feeling continued until we received the instruction to begin offering the phrases to ourselves again. Immediately, I saw my own stuff return with a vengeance.

As the week progressed, we were led with wisdom, humor, and gentleness through many different aspects of the practice, and by the end of the week I felt as if I were sitting more deeply in my own heart. Like chanting, metta is a subtle and deep practice that's particularly well suited for Westerners—designed to help us wish ourselves well. It cuts right to the core of our issues.

If we thought about it, we wouldn't think that wishing ourselves well would be a problem. After all, we all claim to want to be happy. We all try to do things in life that bring us the things we want to have, so it seems like we *are* wishing ourselves well. But when we actually try to find that feeling of well-being inside of us, to taste it directly, we're left with a bitter taste in our mouths. This practice brings up *everything,* all of the places we hide our secret stash of self-judgment.

Doing any spiritual practice is, in a sense, making an offering to ourselves. When we do a practice, we're responsible only for doing that practice—for making the effort, the offering, as deeply as we can. We shouldn't feel like we failed if our lives haven't totally changed after sitting for 20 minutes. When we offer something, we just offer it. When we offer food to somebody who's hungry, we don't sit there and watch him chew it and digest it and see if he's absorbing the vitamins and minerals. Chanting is an offering to the universe.

One time Sharon and I were leading a workshop together in L.A., and it was such a beautiful event that at the end, I said, "Aw jeez, I wish we could all go somewhere where we could all live together." And then I realized, "Wait a minute—we did that. Earth!"

After the workshop, somebody came up to me and asked, "I know what Sharon means when she talks about metta and offering lovingkindness, but what about you? What does that mean for you?" Without thinking, I said, "Hare Krishna!" And I was amazed. When I chant, that's my offering of lovingkindness to the universe. All of these years I'd unconsciously thought that my practice of chanting was something I was doing for myself alone. But now I saw how the effects of chanting rippled out in all directions. I'd thought I was just trying to save my own ass, so to speak. After all, I was sinking in quicksand, up to my nose in it. That's why I started chanting. The thing is that my definition of "my ass" has changed through the doing of the practice.

The more we cultivate, in this moment, the desire to wish ourselves and others well—to do good for the world and for ourselves—the more we're able to allow these good feelings to penetrate into our hearts. Go to the supermarket sometime and push your cart around the aisles, but instead of being asleep like usual, look around. *Nobody's there.* Everybody's on automatic pilot, grabbing stuff and putting it in the cart. There's nobody *present.* Everyone's totally lost in the stuff that's going through their heads. This gives you the chance to walk through the aisles and wish everybody well: *I wish for everybody to be happy and to wake up and have everything they want in life.* It's a wonderful thing to do. By the time you get out of that store, you'll be melting in love.

How we feel about ourselves is what governs the quality of our lives. Practice shouldn't be about trying to be happy-happy-happy all the time without looking at the very causes of our unhappiness. It's about being able to release that tension in the heart. It's about being able to see what another person is going through without feeling like a victim of her processing. It's an absolute possibility to be so at ease in ourselves that when somebody's projecting heavily onto us, we can smile and mentally say, "No, thanks." When we're really relaxed about ourselves and feeling okay, another's negativity melts as it comes toward us. By not reacting and closing her off, we're just naturally helping that individual release her stuff.

When we start to see how we're all interconnected and that we're constantly reacting with everything and everyone around us, we begin to see the truth: until we're all happy, until we're all safe, no one can be completely free of suffering. A bodhisattva is a great being who has recognized the interdependence of all life and sees that because we're constantly locked in action and reaction with each other—with the whole universe—no one is really separate from anyone else and, until we're all free, no one is free. The Bodhisattva Vow is the pledge that Great Beings make to remain available to us until we're all home free.

We start by working for our own happiness because that's what seems most important to us. As we do practice, the way we see ourselves changes radically. Great Beings *know* that we are all One. What a bodhisattva does is what *we* can do. It's not impossible; it just takes practice.

Practice when you're happy, when you're sad, when you're tired, when you're awake; practice when you don't have the time to practice, and when you do have time to practice. You can't think your way out of this stuff. It takes a practice that you do regularly over time to develop the ability to release negativity and cultivate positive qualities.

In the words of Anandamayi Ma:

> If you go on scrubbing a dirty vessel, its own swarup [true form] gradually gets revealed, then you find out whether it is copper, brass, silver, etc. So by repeating God's Name your own swarupa becomes revealed. Therefore, do it all the time, whether you feel like it or not.[15]

DOOR OF FAITH

There is a story about a Tibetan lama who was visiting Burma. At one monastery, he was brought to a temple and told, "Our guru is in here. He sat down to meditate, and he never moved again. Eventually we covered him over with this *stupa* [a stone mound]."

The monks thought this was a wonderful thing, that their guru had reached a very high state. But the lama shook his head and said, "Oh, that's too bad."

Surprised, the monks asked, "What do you mean?"

"He learned to meditate, but he never learned how to live."

The point of a practice is to give us the strength to live in a positive way, to have a good quality of life—a good quality of *internal* life—not to get lost in what might be a temporary, albeit long-lasting, subtle meditative state. In order to live in a more peaceful internal environment, the ability to let go of our thoughts is crucial. And in order to release thoughts, we have to be able to turn our attention away from them, so we need to turn our attention toward something else. One of the most effective methods is to turn our attention to the flow of the Name. By practicing the repetition of the Name, we develop the ability to release those thoughts and enter into a deeper, calmer space. We have to do it billions of times, but with every repetition, our ability gets stronger.

There are certain practices and traditions where mantras are used to accomplish a particular objective. These mantras have to be orally transmitted, and the words need to be pronounced accurately. If we want to stop a train, for example, there's a mantra for that. If we want to get rich, there are mantras for that. Those things need to be taught and repeated correctly. But the Name of God is our own true nature. We can call our partner "Honey," "Sweetheart," "Cookie," or a million other names, but the same person will respond. It's not something we have to be taught. We *become* it by going deeply into ourselves.

From turning toward the deepest place in ourselves, everything else that we want in life—our "beneficial desires," or the things that help us in our lives—eventually comes to us. They say that Hanuman not only bestows liberation, but also gives us everything we need: all of our beneficial desires, the things that will be helpful to us on the path of our lives.

Shirdi Sai Baba, a great saint who left his body in 1918, used to say, "I give people what they want in the hopes that someday they'll want what I want to give them." We need to get what we want to some extent. We need to satisfy our basic hungers or we won't be able to focus on finding something deeper. As Maharaj-ji was fond of noting, "You can't talk to a hungry man about God. Feed him first."

A certain amount of so-called success in life shows us a lot about ourselves, because if we keep our eyes open, we'll see that getting what we wanted hasn't given us the deeper feeling that we were looking for. Through the repetition of the Name, all of the desires that are useful for us on the path will be fulfilled, and the things that hurt us will be removed. That's what Maharaj-ji said, and I believe him. Maharaj-ji was not talking from our limited worldly point of view. He knew what he was talking about.

He also said, "Go ahead, keep singing your lying *Ram Ram,* your false *Ram Ram.* Go ahead, keep singing. One of these days you'll say it right *once,* and you'll be free." What does that mean? Why is it a false *Ram Ram?* Maybe because we're doing the practice without real devotion and love.

One time somebody asked Maharaj-ji, "Should I repeat God's Name even though I have no faith and no feelings of devotion?"

And he replied, "Well, what will you do? Something is better than nothing. To begin with, one may not be entirely sincere, but over time, the heart opens and a pure longing arises. Can anyone see God with human eyes? One must have divine sight to see Him, and a person only gets it after purification of the heart. For this, leading a good life, prayer, and spiritual practice are essential. Go on reciting *Ram Ram,* and one day you will call Him with your whole heart and you will be saved."

One night a man was crying,
Allah! Allah!
His lips grew sweet with praising,
until a cynic said,
"So! I have heard you calling out, but have you ever
gotten any response?"

The man had no answer to that.
He quit praying and fell into a confused sleep.

He dreamed he saw Khidr, the guide of souls,
in a thick, green foliage.
"Why did you stop praising?"
"Because I've never heard anything back."
"This longing you express is the return message."

The grief you cry out from
draws you toward union.

*Your pure sadness
that wants help
is the secret cup.*

*Listen to the moan of a dog for its master.
That whining is the connection.*

*There are love dogs
no one knows the names of.*

*Give your life
to be one of them.*

— Rumi[16]

We tend to hear the Name only with our outer senses, not with our inner awareness. In the West, a name describes something's outward appearance—we look around and see what's on the outside, and we name it. In India, they say that the name and what is named are not different. We Westerners are so distracted that we can't penetrate to the deeper reality. We say *Ram Ram,* but we don't know what it's the name of; in this sense, it's indeed a false *Ram Ram.* The proof that we're saying the Name falsely is that we're not having the deepest experience of reality when we say it.

For instance, the mantra *Om* is repeated at the beginning of so many spiritual events. *Om* is the totality of the universe—the sound/vibration of all of the billions of beings and things that make up the whole universe. It is the "Word" mentioned in the Bible. But when we chant *Om,* do we have a direct experience of "the Word was with God, and the Word was God"? No. That's what Maharaj-ji called the false *Ram Ram.* It is in the Name, in the *Om,* but we just don't yet get it.

Once, my friend Sri Sacinandana Swami said, "You should become like a leaf on the river of the Name, with no will of your own, moving by the power and will of the river. *Japa* [repetition of the Name] should be done not just with the mouth, nor just with the mind, but with a loving heart."

I asked, "But how do Westerners find that loving feeling within when our hearts have been so crushed by life?"

He replied, "The Name will purify and clean your heart of its scars of betrayal and abuse. Then the love that resides in your own heart can be revealed."

ᚠᛘ ᛚᛁᚼᛉᛘᚼᛁᚢ ᛉᛁᚼ ᛏᛁᚼ

At first we may only have a slim hope that spiritual practice of lovingkindness will work for us. But the more we feel some small movement in our life—a change, a shift in direction, maybe some lightening up—the more our hope will develop into confidence, and eventually into faith. Comedian George Carlin used to do a famous sketch about the words that can't be said on television because some people find them offensive. Over the years, I've compiled a similar list of words that make Westerners uncomfortable. At the top of the list is *faith.*

Faith, as we hear the word used in the West, implies belief in something outside of ourselves that cannot be proven or experienced by us directly; it has to be taken on . . . faith. On the path of dharma, the path that leads to true freedom, faith has nothing to do with blind belief, but is rather a very personal understanding that what we're seeking, what we're longing for, actually exists and can be found. This very small amount of faith is all that's necessary to begin to awaken. If we're involved with the so-called spiritual path at all, there is already something tugging at us—a longing for a deeper love, a yearning to find a haven for our hearts. Somewhere in us, hidden even from our conscious mind, we have faith. They say that as human beings, we experience being pulled into our own hearts, by our own hearts, as "longing."

Faith and hope are two different things. Although we may *hope* that things will change for the better, we may not really believe it's possible. Let's say we find ourselves confined in a totally dark room. We have no idea where we are or how we got there. We have no idea if there is a way out at all, but we certainly hope so. All of a sudden, the lights come on for a second, and we see a door. This is the moment when our lives begin to change. For me, that door was meeting Ram Dass. It was, simply put, the awakening of faith. It can come to us in many ways, but when it comes, it changes everything. That's because, even after the lights go out again, we know that there *is* a door, and we won't rest until we find it.

Faith is based on our own experience, not on what somebody told us or something we read. *This feels right. I'll do it.* From my own direct experience, I began to realize that there's truth in the practice of the Name. I don't know the whole truth, by far, and I've made many mistakes. But after a while I learned to trust that through the practice of chanting, I've developed more ability to be *here* and I'll be able to deal with anything that comes up, even though I may still be afraid. This is the strength that comes from practice, the confidence in ourselves that is the fruit of practice.

And when I look at my teachers, I see that place of calm confidence in them. I see where they must be coming from, what their experience must be like in order for them to be able to transmit such strength and wisdom. They fully trust themselves. They know to a much greater degree than I what reality is and that there really is a good way to live in the world. When I trust their experience, it gives me more faith—real living faith.

As Saint Paul said, "By grace was I saved though faith." That's why Maharaj-ji told the guy to just keep repeating the Name. So just keep doing your practice, even if you feel that you have no devotion. Just the doing of it *is* devotion. Through the constant repetition of these Names, the presence that's hidden within us is uncovered. The jewel is already there, it's just covered up with our stuff. These practices don't *give* us ourselves, they *uncover* ourselves.

Caught in the storm, battered by waves
The ship of my life was blown off course
By the winds of selfishness . . .

My breath rises within me,
the breath of the heart.
The sweet breath.
The sacred breath leads me in.

Now the winds begin to die down
and the waters grow calm.
I have found a haven for my heart,
In the Harbor of the Name.

— Krishna Das

The story of Ramana Maharshi gives us more faith in what is possible. Ramana Maharshi was a saint who left his body in 1950. His father died when he was a boy, and he went to live with his uncle. He was a regular kid and student who played with the other children. One day, however, he was sitting by himself in his uncle's living room when he felt as if he were going to die. The imminence of death drove his mind inward. He asked himself:

> *Now that death has come; what does it mean? What is it that is dying? Only this body dies.* And at once I dramatized the occurrence of death. I held my breath and kept my lips tightly closed and said to myself, *This body is dead. It will be carried to the cremation ground and reduced to ashes. But with the death of this body, am I dead? Is this body "I"? I am the spirit transcending the body. That means I am the deathless* atman [Universal Self].[17]

At that moment, he had full realization of the Self, of God.

Later Ramana Maharshi said that since that moment, "My awareness has never changed from total awareness in the Self, total residing in the truth." He left home and found his way to a sacred hill in southern India named Arunachala, which has been worshipped for many thousands of years as a living form of Shiva. Eventually his devotees built a simple ashram for him there, and he spent the rest of his life around that hill. When he was dying, his devotees cried, "Oh, Bhagavan, you're leaving us!"

He just looked at them with much compassion and said, "Where could I go? I am here."

When Ramana Maharshi's mother found him in Arunachala many years after he'd disappeared from home, she wanted to take him back with her. He told her:

> The Ordainer controls the fate of souls in accordance with their *prarabdha-karma* [the destiny to be worked out in this life resulting from a balance sheet of actions in past lives]. Whatever is destined not to happen will not happen, try hard as you may. Whatever is destined to happen will happen, do what you may to prevent it. This is certain. The best course, therefore, is to remain silent.[18]

This is a very deep statement. The first thing to realize is that he's saying that what's happening now is the result of past actions, and what's going to happen in the future includes how we act in this very moment. Simply put, everything has a cause. Happiness has a cause; unhappiness has a cause. Some causes are easily understood and some are not. This is the basis of what's called karma. The laws of karma are very subtle, but it's obvious that if the thoughts we're having now are like waves that were caused by a storm far out at sea in our own past, then the way we meet these waves will affect how far and how long they travel. If we get bounced around uncontrollably by them, we're actually producing more waves. If we find some way not to react, we can calm the waves, and then we're creating a more peaceful present as well as future.

When Ramana Maharshi counsels us to "remain silent," he doesn't mean "don't speak." He's referring to the great silence of the Self, of God. He's telling us to remain at ease in the presence of God, our own true Self, and to deal with whatever arises in our lives from this deep place of realization. First, of course, we have to find that presence. For that, much effort and much grace is needed. The point is that it can be found. And it doesn't matter where we live or what our life may look like.

To quote Saint John of the Cross:

> The Father uttered one Word; that Word is His Son: and He utters Him for ever in everlasting silence, and in silence the soul has to hear It.[19]

Many Westerners try to bend themselves into an Eastern shape, imagining that it's more spiritual. Stories of yogis with magical powers, meditating for years in caves, fascinate us. What we don't realize is that if we were supposed to be living in a cave, we'd already be there. If we're obsessing about dropping everything and running off to live in a cave in the Himalayas, there's no use going. If we went off to a cave right now, we'd bring everything with us. Our minds aren't going to stop because we don't have a TV. With no one around and nothing else to distract us, we're really going to see ourselves and our stuff, but we won't have the tools to deal with what we see. So what's the sense?

Renunciation is another word that Westerners misunderstand. Renunciation does not mean neurotic self-denial. Another word for renunciation is *vairagya,* which translates as "the natural falling away of worldliness or the fascination with external things." Maharaj-ji often said that when the time is right, attachment will fall away. He rarely asked people to give up doing things they were attached to, even if those things could be harmful to them. Everything in our life is there for a reason. We may not know what those reasons are, and we may have trouble dealing with those things, but they're there for a reason. Many householders who are married with families realize God—it's not something that solely happens to monks and celibates. It's just a different path leading to the same goal. It's love flowing into love.

Ramana Maharshi was a *gyani,* one who follows the path of self-awareness, or knowledge. He said that gyanis experience *after* enlightenment what a *bhakta* (a follower of the path of devotion) experiences on the way *to* enlightenment, on the way to merging. One goes one direction and has all that bliss and love after the journey is completed, and one has it along the way. But it's all the same. It's all One.

"All One." *(Courtesy of Balaram Das.)*

Many times we'd be sitting with Maharaj-ji, and he'd look at us and hold up one finger, as if he were calling us out on something. We knew that he knew everything—past, present, and future— so we couldn't imagine what we were getting busted for. Was it something we did, were doing, or were going to do? So one day someone just up and asked, "Maharaj-ji, what does it mean when you do that?"

By way of explanation, he looked at us intensely and held up his "pointer" finger in front of us. Then he held up all five fingers, one by one, shook them around and held up that one finger again. He said, "Many names, many forms . . . *sab ek,* all One."

All One. This was his bottom line. All One. One being, one world and all of the people living in it, one family. Maharaj-ji said it over and over again—*sab ek. All One.* There's only one of us. It's like we're the cells of this huge body, and each cell is healing itself. Gradually, but inevitably, the whole body will heal. It might take 40 billion light years, but that's where we're going. One cell at a time. One heart at a time. Yours. Mine. Each one of us. All One.

A wave on the ocean is made up of nothing but water. The surface of the ocean gets blown by the wind, and forms what we call waves. On one level this is perfectly understandable, but it's also true that the wave is, and never was, anything but the water. When we identify with the wave, we believe *I am a wave.* When we identify with the water, there is only water, and waveness is seen as relatively real. As humans, we identify with the body/wave and feel separate from other bodies/waves. When we go deeper into ourselves, we're freed of that thinking and experience being the ocean of Oneness. Chanting brings us closer to the realization of the way things actually are right beneath the surface because the Names come from the place *beneath* the waves.

The One, the Self, God, the pure awareness that is looking out through your eyes at me is the same pure awareness that is looking out through my eyes at you. But Oneness doesn't mean that we don't honor our individuality. The more conscious we are of the Oneness, the more our individual lives reflect that awareness. We're no longer only concerned with our small, separate, individual world, so more harmonious qualities can flow into our lives.

We can't think our way out of feeling separate, but when we do a practice, the walls we've constructed around our hearts begin to get broken down. We become more ourselves, not less. What do we lose except fear and unhappiness? Everything that has held us back or limited us begins to disappear from our lives. We become peace. No effort is needed to hold it. That's love. Real love. That's *heart.* That place, that presence, is heart. It's not a *feeling* that comes and goes—it's who we *are.*

I once asked a saint whom I was visiting, "How can I get closer to my guru?" He looked at me as if I were crazy, and replied, "Your guru is what's looking through your eyes right now."

> *Let your thoughts flow past you, calmly;*
> *keep me near, at every moment;*
> *trust me with your life, because I*
> *am you, more than you yourself are.*

— the Bhagavad Gita[20]

For me, Maharaj-ji is this presence of love, this space of love. When I was with him physically, it was *only* there, in that body. But now that love is everywhere. Anywhere I look, when I look, I can find it. And when I sing, I don't necessarily hold his physical form in my mind; I sing to this *now*—to *here,* to this presence of love. And the presence opens up and gets deeper and deeper and deeper.

It's a deeper version of *us,* deeper than who we know ourselves to be. We become *more* ourselves. We sit more comfortably in ourselves, more relaxed, more at ease. It can't be anywhere else than where we are. It *can't* be. And so it's always present. Learning to be ourselves, seeing life as our teacher rather than as something that happens to us, all this is based on the faith that there *is* something to learn and something to become. As the ancient saying goes:

> *Without grace, no faith.*
> *Without faith, no surrender.*
> *Without the guru, no grace.*

Dada at home in Allahabad, 1980s.

FOLLOWING IN THE FOOTPRINTS
OF LOVE: DADA

*T*here are those we can learn from, solid examples of faith and devotion. If we know anything about a path at all, it's only because of the great beings who have gone before us. Out of their love, out of their kindness, they left footprints for us to follow, the footprints of love. Besides spending time with my guru, I've been fortunate to have met many of the great saints of my generation. I bow to each one of them and thank them for who they are and the way they've inspired me. I've also had the wonderful opportunity to spend a lot of time with the old devotees of Maharaj-ji—many of whom had known him for most of their lives—who shared their love and wisdom with me freely in the many years after he left his body.

Sudhir Mukerjee, whom Maharaj-ji called Dada, was one of the leading economics professors at the University of Allahabad in India. Before he met Maharaj-ji, he didn't believe in God or participate in any religious activities or rituals. And then one day

Dada's wife, Kamala (who was called *Didi*, "elder sister"), was leaving the house to go out. Dada was sitting with his friends and asked where she was going. She said that a baba had come to the house across the street, and she was going for his darshan. As soon as the baba saw Didi, he told her to leave. She didn't want to, so she sat there. After a minute or two, the baba again told her to go, but she didn't. Then he called her by name, "Kamala, your husband's Bengali friends have come. Go serve them tea. I shall come tomorrow morning." So she had to leave. When she returned home and told Dada what had happened, he was amazed and became very curious. He decided to go visit the baba himself the next morning.

The next day, as soon as Dada entered the house where the baba was staying, the baba got up, took his hand, and started walking very fast across the street. Entering Dada's home, the baba said, "From now on, I will be staying with you." To use one of Dada's favorite phrases, "Can you imagine that!" This is what is called lila!

The baba was Maharaj-ji, and from that time on, whenever he was in Allahabad he stayed at Dada's house. Over the course of time, Dada was transformed into one of his closest and most dear devotees. Dada even wrote two books about his life with Maharaj-ji—*By His Grace* and *The Near and the Dear*—in which he speaks a lot about the older devotees of Maharaj-ji who took him under their wing. It was from them that Dada learned about devotion and how to be a devotee.

It was much the same for me and many of the other Westerners. The depth of Dada's love and devotion for Maharaj-ji was bottomless, and stories about Maharaj-ji's lilas would flow from him like a river in the rainy season. We would bathe in the sweetness, humor, and joy that spread in all directions when Dada spoke. There was always a new story to be told, but even the ones that I'd heard a hundred times before brought me deeply into my guru's presence, time and time again.

One summer, Dada was staying at Kainchi during his break from teaching at the university. He'd be with Maharaj-ji all day. At this time, Dada was still smoking cigarettes. Every once in a while, Maharaj-ji would look at him and make a motion like he was smoking and say, "Dada, go and take your two minutes." Two of the other Westerners who lived in the temple and I would be waiting for him in one of our rooms. We had chai ready and his favorite brand of cigarettes, along with an ashtray. Dada would arrive and start drinking and smoking and telling Maharaj-ji stories. It was bliss. Then he'd suddenly stop midsentence. His head would turn toward the front of the temple, and he'd throw the cigarette down. *Then* we'd hear Maharaj-ji calling, *"Dada!"* It happened many times like that. Dada felt Maharaj-ji's call heading in his direction and was already on his way out the door by the time his voice reached our ears.

During the years I was in India, Maharaj-ji stayed at Dada's house on Church Lane in Allahabad during the winter months, his "winter camp" as it was called. Many of the Western devotees spent some of the winter months nearby, having darshan and being fed humongous amounts of food by the devotees there. It was like the Grand Central Station of love, with devotees coming and going all day and kirtan going on continuously. Everyone was smiling and happy to be near Maharaj-ji.

During this time, Maharaj-ji was calling me "Driver," and I carried the keys to the Volkswagen bus with me all the time. I secretly hoped that one day I'd have the opportunity to drive Maharaj-ji somewhere. Sure enough, as soon as I walked in Dada's door one afternoon, Maharaj-ji asked me if I had the keys.

When I told him I did, he said, "Let's go."

We walked out of the house and up to the VW bus. Dada was holding Maharaj-ji's hand and opened the passenger door for him. The seat was high, so he kind of threw himself up into it, and as he did, he bashed his head on the door frame really hard. I started freaking out, shouting, *"Dada!* Did you see that?!"

As he closed the door for Maharaj-ji, Dada looked at me and

simply said, "He did it on purpose. Now drive." That's devotion! You see, in Dada's world, everything that happened was Maharaj-ji's doing, and anything that Maharaj-ji did, he did purposely. He accepted everything as Maharaj-ji's prasad, his offering. If someone arrived, it was because Maharaj-ji had called him. If someone left it, was because Maharaj-ji had sent him away.

By the time I met him, Dada was a "fully baked" devotee and had no doubt that Maharaj-ji was God in human form. That may seem a little extreme to most Westerners, but for Dada, it was Maharaj-ji's world, and everything and everyone danced to his tune.

On the devotional path, to be completely immersed in the Loving Presence is called *surrender*. We don't "do" surrender; it happens as we ripen in love. Surrender is the same as being fully in the moment. Maharaj-ji used to say, "Guru, God, and Self are one." To truly be *here* means that we're residing in that awareness. We deal with whatever comes from *that* place, seeing and accepting everything as is. This doesn't mean we don't try to change the things that need changing, but our actions come from a very different place—a place free from fear or expectation. If we still worry and have tension and anxiety, then we haven't surrendered. If the mind has not stopped its obsessive chattering and we still believe everything it tells us, we haven't surrendered. Surrender is the goal of the path of devotion. For me, surrender means being lost in love.

Anyway, Maharaj-ji was obviously fine, so I got in the car and off we went. I was so excited! He said to drive toward the *Sangam,* the holy confluence of three sacred rivers (the Ganges, the Yamuna, and the invisible river, Sarasvati) and the place where the big melas are held. The whole time I was driving, Maharaj-ji was acting like he was really nervous and scared. "Watch out! Watch out! Slow down! Be careful! See that guy over there? Be careful. Don't hit him!" And on and on. We finally reached the mela grounds, and as soon as I stopped the car, he said, "Okay, let's go back." I turned the car around and drove back to the house. That was that. It was the only time I got to drive him.

Sometime after this, Ram Dass, two other devotees, and I were driving to Delhi from Allahabad. I was behind the wheel when we came to a very long curve that was right beside a reservoir. I realized that I was going way too fast; the car would never make the turn, and we might keep going right into the water. Just at that moment, a strong wind blew us back to safety on the right side of the road. I immediately remembered Maharaj-ji banging his head on the car. I felt that he had known what would happen and had saved us from certain death.

In the years after Maharaj-ji left his body, I spent a lot of time with Dada, staying at the house on Church Lane. It was a blessing to be able to hang out with him, especially when all he talked about was Maharaj-ji. He was totally immersed in Maharaj-ji's love. To hang out with him was intoxicating and uplifting, and it opened up new channels for the love to flow. The intensity of his devotion to Maharaj-ji was contagious, and I was infected with it. It showed me that it was possible to live deeply in love and that one needed no special "credentials." Dada was simply a human being who radiated extraordinary love and kindness to all of us who came in Maharaj-ji's name.

At one point when I was staying with him, Dada must have felt that I was reverencing him too much. He said, "Krishna Das, I may be a step or two ahead of you, and you may be a step or two ahead of others, but we are all on this side—only he has gone beyond."

Another time when I arrived at Dada's house in Allahabad, he got the key to the bedroom and I followed him upstairs. By now he was more than 80 years old and moved very slowly. As we reached the top of the stairway, he sighed, "Oh, Krishna Das, it's so hard to come up . . . so hard to come up." Then as he put the key in the door, he turned with a mischievous smile and said, "So easy to go down." We both laughed. He was playing with me, teasing me about getting an inflated spiritual ego.

In 1989 I came to Allahabad with the intention of staying at the Kumbh Mela, in the camp of a saint I'd met. I came early so that I could spend a few days at Dada's house before going to the mela. Dada couldn't understand why I'd want to stay at the mela or spend time with any saint besides Maharaj-ji, but he didn't say anything. On the day I was to move to the mela grounds, the saint sent one of his disciples to bring me and some other Westerners to the camp. The disciple was very full of himself and arrogant. He was also very disrespectful to Dada, who was his elder by far.

Dada grabbed me, pulled me into the room he kept for Maharaj-ji, and closed the door. He said, "Krishna Das, I must show you something." There was an old *almirah* (cupboard) in the room, and he reached way up on top of it in the back and took down an old key. He opened the almirah and reached down to the back of the bottom shelf, taking out something that was wrapped in an old dirty cloth. He held it in front of me and, with great intensity, asked, "Do you see?"

"No. See what?"

He unwrapped it, revealing a dull, beat-up, cheap aluminum *lota* (small pot). Looking deeply into my eyes, he replied, "He left this for me when he went away. Do you see? Do you see?"

"No, Dada, I don't see."

He looked at me with a mad glint in his eye and said, "You don't have to shine. *You don't have to shine.*"

Then Dada wrapped the lota in the dirty cloth, placed it again at the back of the bottom shelf, closed and locked the doors of the almirah, hid the key in its place on top, and walked out of the room. He left me standing there, with "You don't have to shine" ringing in my ears. I can never forget that. It was his way of pointing out the arrogance of that disciple. Once again, Dada was teaching me that true love expresses itself with humility; it isn't something that makes us bright and shiny to the world. True spirituality makes one softhearted and humble. It doesn't make one glimmer on the surface and all puffed up with self-importance. A cup doesn't have to be made of gold to be filled with the nectar of love.

One year the Tewaris and I had been visiting Dada, and the Tewaris were waiting in the car to leave when Dada called me to his room. He was holding a book about a great woman saint named Anandamayi Ma. He showed me a picture of the author, who was himself a very respected sadhu. Then he leafed through the book until he found the page he was looking for and said, "Read this."

Here's what I saw:

> In the early 1980s, I was staying with Mataji [Anandamayi Ma] in one of her ashrams and we went to visit Neem Karoli Baba, who was living in a cave nearby and hiding from His devotees. We brought Him back to the ashram where He spent a few days with us before returning to his cave.

At this moment, Tewari came in the house, upset that I'd kept them waiting in the car. I told him to read the same paragraph.

After he did, he told me, "There's nothing surprising about that. Maharaj-ji and Mataji knew each other very well."

"Baba, this was in 1982."

"So?"

"Baba, Maharaj-ji died in 1973."

"Oh!" His face turned pale. At that point, Dada took the book and put it away, and we got in the car and drove back to Lucknow. This incident taught me two things. First of all, it was clear that Dada's understanding and appreciation of Maharaj-ji was far beyond my own limited view, and that the scope of Maharaj-ji's work in this world could never be fully understood.

The second thing I learned was in some ways even more amazing. If I had any inkling that Maharaj-ji was somehow magically still living in a physical body somewhere, I'd be running like a madman through the jungles trying to find him. The fact that Dada believed that he was still in a body and wasn't going crazy trying to find him demonstrated the depth of his surrender. He was content to take what Maharaj-ji gave him and wasn't concerned with anything other than living in his loving presence. This was a very humbling lesson for me.

Many times I'd hang out on the porch with Dada late into the night. He'd sit there, smoking his cigarettes and staring out into the dark. Sitting in silence with him, I'd try to "tune in" to his flow of devotion. As I did, I'd see mini-movies of Maharaj-ji playing in my head. I realized that Dada was fully immersed in the thoughts of his Beloved. I prayed that I could be like that someday.

LOVE—SERVE—REMEMBER

Growing up on Long Island, there definitely was no one like Dada in my life. When I was 17, I used to hang out (illegally) in a bar with some friends. One night I got really drunk on Singapore Slings and wrote my first poem:

> *Into the mirror I will go*
> *To find the me others know.*
> *Out of the mirror I will come*
> *Reassured that I am one.*

I had such low self-esteem and such a scrambled sense of who I was that I thought I could find myself if I could just see how others saw me. But even then, feeling as lost as I did, I was always looking for something. What I had to learn was how to get lost in love, and I'd been given a good example of someone who *was* lost in love: Jesus Christ.

Imagine my surprise when Maharaj-ji started talking to us Westerners about Jesus. He'd tell us things like, "Hanuman and Christ are the same." Terrific. Just great! That's why I left Long Island? To go ten thousand miles to the Himalayas to hear that?

As Lama Surya Das says, I grew up Jewish on my parents' side, so I didn't really have much feeling for Jesus. As a child I'd get up early to watch cartoons on Sunday and, as I'd go through the channels, I'd see those guys pounding on that black book and yelling at people in his name. I also remember the day when all of my Catholic friends came back from their first confirmation class and told me that I killed Jesus. I didn't remember killing anybody! That was the end of it for me and organized religion. It was only disorganized religion from then on.

So it was quite a shock when Maharaj-ji began to talk to us about Christ. At first we Westerners thought it was because it was the "local religion" where we came from, but he spoke with such sweetness and depth of emotion that we decided we should read the Bible ourselves. So one Sunday morning we got together; put on our white, holy clothes; sat out on the porch of the Evelyn Hotel, where we were staying; and read the Gospels out loud. They sounded very different up there in the Himalayas. *Very* different. It was amazing. The love that Jesus was talking about was the same kind of love that our guru was talking about. The same love, the same power of truth, the compassion, and the zero tolerance for bullshit were what we were feeling for the first time in India with Maharaj-ji, and because of him we recognized that it was the same with Jesus. We were with somebody who loved us in a way we couldn't have imagined, much in the same way in which Jesus loved his people.

One day a Canadian man arrived for his first darshan. He didn't know much about Maharaj-ji but had heard about him from Ram Dass. Maharaj-ji didn't give lectures or formal teachings; didn't write books; and, as far as I know, didn't formally initiate people. He just kept shining like the sun. Flowers don't need to read a manual on how to bloom in the sunshine. So when Maharaj-ji asked this man why he'd come and what he wanted, he was unsure how to respond. Finally, he replied, "Can you teach me how to meditate?"

Maharaj-ji's response was: "Meditate like Christ. Go. Sit in the back of the temple with the other Westerners."

The guy came to the back, and we asked him about his darshan. He told us that Maharaj-ji had said to meditate like Christ. At first we were surprised. "What! Meditate like Christ! What does that mean?" But then we thought about it. We were always trying to get Maharaj-ji to tell us what practice to do, but he'd never give us any specific instructions about yoga or meditation. Now he'd said this. If he said it, he must know how Jesus meditated. We decided to ask him about it. We were so excited—we were going to get the secret teachings at last!

Later in the day, when Maharaj-ji came to the back of the temple to hang out with us, Ram Dass broached the subject that had us all buzzing. "You said to meditate like Christ. How *did* he meditate?"

It seemed as if Maharaj-ji was about to answer, but instead his eyes closed and he sat there completely still, completely silent. It felt like he'd totally disappeared. In all the time I'd been with him, I'd only seen him sitting motionless like this a couple of times before. It was extraordinarily powerful, as if the whole universe had become silent. Then a tear came down his cheek. We were in awe. After a couple of minutes, his eyes half opened and, with great emotion, he quietly said, "He lost himself in love, that's how he meditated. He was one with all beings. He loved everyone, even the people who crucified him. He never died. He is the *atman* [soul]. He lives in the hearts of all. He lost himself in love."

Once again, Maharaj-ji had gone right to the heart of it all. I was stunned. There was nothing I wanted more than to be able to lose myself in love, but there was nothing that seemed farther away.

It is easy to bear the heat of fire and likewise
it is possible to tread the edge of the sword.
But to sustain an unchanging love is a most difficult business.

— Kabir[21]

Because he said it, I knew it was true. Because he said it, I knew it was possible. And that was a big difference. It changed the way I thought about meditation. Up until then, I'd felt that meditation was like wrestling with my own mind, with no clear feeling of direction. Now I saw that everything that was happening with Maharaj-ji and in my life was leading to that very place—the ability to lose myself in love. And, of course, that's where Maharaj-ji lives.

In the Bhagavad Gita, Sri Krishna, speaking as the embodiment of that place, says:

> *And when he sees me in all and sees all in me,*
> *Then I never leave him and he never leaves me.*
> *And he, who in this oneness of love*
> *Loves me in whatever he sees,*
> *Wherever this man may live,*
> *In truth, he lives in me . . .*

The problem is that everything they write in those books is *all true*. It's a problem because it means that there really is something to find, and it's up to us to do so. It's the essence of every single thing we look and long for in our lives. When we have it here, we have it *everywhere*. When we don't have it in here, we don't have it *anywhere*. And to the amount and extent that we have it inside, that's how much we see it outside. There's no difference between our "spiritual" life and "regular" life.

One day Maharaj-ji said to Mr. Tewari, "So, you're a Brahmin, you're supposed to know everything. Tell me, what did Krishna teach in the Gita?"

Tewari knew it was a setup and there was no escape, but he gave the answer most people would give: "He taught *nishkama karma*, selfless service or 'desireless action.'"

Maharaj-ji yelled, "You miserable Brahmins, always misleading the people! Only God can do selfless service."

Another time Maharaj-ji instructed, "Go on following the trodden path faithfully by thought, word, and action. Only then will God reside in your heart and you will be able to perform nishkama karma. The ability to do nishkama karma can be achieved only by His grace and cannot be acquired by any other means. None can claim a right to His grace. It is up to Him to give it, to refuse it, or to take it away."

This is a deep subject. Maharaj-ji spoke all the time about serving others, but he never mentioned the words *karma yoga*. He never encouraged us to think about "self-centered" spiritual practice—practices that are meant to achieve some spiritual benefit for ourselves—he just said to care for others. He never told us to meditate. When we asked him how to find God, he said, "Serve people."

We didn't understand. So we asked, "How do we raise *kundalini* [spiritual energy that rests at the base of the spine]?"

He said, "Feed people and remember God."

It was confusing to me at that time because I was so sure I needed to do some special practice or get some secret mantra in order to cure myself of my unhappiness. Of course, all I really needed was to stop thinking about myself *all the time.*

Giving a hungry person some food is the most natural thing to do, but it's hard to come out from behind the walls of our fears. There's a tendency to make a big deal about it and create a whole ego trip of being a person who's doing good. Of course, there is a spiritual benefit that comes to us from alleviating other people's hunger and pain. As Maharaj-ji said, it raises kundalini. But if our motive is to get the benefit more than to alleviate pain, then we miss the real benefit: tasting the love that comes when the walls of separateness break down and we experience our deep connection with other people.

One day we Westerners were sitting across the courtyard from Maharaj-ji, being fed mounds of puris and potatoes. Maharaj-ji turned to Dada and said, "I'm eating through all those mouths." From where he was sitting, it didn't matter whose mouth the food went in because there is only one of us.

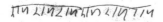

"Do unto others as you would have them do unto you." That's the whole ball game. There's not a second sentence to that. There's nothing else we have to know, nothing more we have to do. This teaching is not about being a "do-gooder" for the sake of others at the expense of our own happiness. It's a spiritual practice that can transform our hearts. If we could simply follow this "golden rule," our whole lives would be filled with love. If we treated other people the way we wanted them to treat us, the quality of our daily lives would shift 180 degrees immediately.

In the words of Shirdi Sai Baba:

> Whoever or whatever creature comes to you, do not drive away but receive with due consideration. Give food to the hungry, water to the thirsty, and clothes to the naked. . . . Bear with others' reproach. Speak only gentle words. This is the way to happiness. . . . The world maintains a wall—the wall of differentiation between oneself and others, between you and me. Destroy this wall.[22]

Everything that human beings do has some motive, some desire attached to it, even if it is the desire to help others and remove some of their suffering. These are positive desires, which can purify our hearts even more, but it's easy to get caught in identifying oneself as the doer of these "good deeds," and then the ego grows stronger. As Maharaj-ji said, only when God comes to reside in our hearts can we really serve people. By doing practices like chanting, our hearts begin to open and God/Love begins to shine brightly. Over time we lose some of our feeling of distance from others, our fear of "others." Then we can begin to feel their suffering as if it were our own.

One thing I can tell you: if we're angry and don't know how to love ourselves—or don't know how to accept love on a personal level—we're seriously limiting our ability to do any good for anybody else. This is not about avoiding social action. This is about getting better at doing anything we choose to do with our lives. The path of dharma is not about getting some personal high that we're going to try to hold on to. We can't just go sit in our bedroom, close the door, do some more chanting, and stay high forever. That's impossible. This is about finding out what it means to be a human being, to be one of *many* human beings in a world where there's incredible suffering.

I've met saints who can raise people from the dead, who know everything we've ever done, who can protect us and save us from all kinds of stuff in our lives, but . . . *they can't make us love ourselves.* That is something *we* have to do.

If things aren't going our way, it doesn't mean we're bad. It doesn't mean we don't deserve happiness. Through practices like chanting, we begin to get in touch with a different place inside of ourselves. There's a goodness, a beauty, and a love that lives in our own hearts—it's who we are when we're not busy convincing ourselves we're not. The better we feel about ourselves, the more our hearts become available to the true love that is our own true nature. If we're really caught in something and giving ourselves a hard time and can't find a way out, we can make the choice to go work in a soup kitchen or do some other service that will open our eyes to the suffering of others that is all around us. Then our own problems don't feel so big and important.

I've found as time goes on that when I feel okay about myself for even a little while, I get more and more sensitive to the suffering of others. And then I want to do more and more to help. This is hard because people aren't always nice; they don't act the way we want them to. But that's all right. We don't have to smile and pin a button on our fellow humans or give them flowers; we just have to let them be who they are. One of the ways to dissolve the separation between ourselves and others is ✳ to cultivate this attitude of caring about people and accepting who they are. Acting in a caring way toward others can begin to break down many barriers in our own hearts.

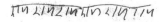

Practices like chanting work by gradually removing our false sense of separateness. It's not *real* separateness; it's a temporary experience. The sense of "me-ness" is a wall, and no wall can last forever. What goes away is everything that keeps us separate, our false identification with our stuff. While we're separate, we're locked up in ourselves. Then everybody is either an object of desire or an object of aversion or fear. It's kind of intense to be locked up in that place all the time, but that's pretty much all we know. We've got to untie that knot in our hearts that believes our personal happiness is separate from, and more important than, the happiness of other people.

We've been trained to think of ourselves first, and where has it gotten us? If we thought of our Self first—the one great Self of which we're all a part—our unhappiness would disappear. But we have to discover for ourselves what that is. It's like when we're listening to really great music, we can forget that we stubbed our toe and it's throbbing. When our attention is on the repetition of the Name, we're not as focused on our own pain or discomfort. We enter into a different relationship with the constant flow of thoughts and then we're just *here*. Our hearts get wider and we don't think as much about my happiness versus your happiness; we care less about ourselves and our own stuff. Those heavy states of mind gradually pass away and are replaced by a more buoyant sense of contentment.

As Sharon Salzberg writes, we have to develop "a heart as wide as the world"—a heart so open that there's room for everything and everyone in the world to fit inside it. Ram Dass speaks of loving the soul or inner being of a person, while not necessarily approving of that person's actions. The crux of developing that kind of heart is learning to be good to ourselves. When we let all of the suffering and sadness in the world destroy us, it doesn't help the world in any way. It's endless.

A reporter once asked the Dalai Lama, "Your Holiness, why does everybody love you so much?" He replied, "I don't know. Maybe it's because I've spent my whole life caring about, and considering the happiness of, other people." Think about that: "Maybe it's because I've spent my whole life"—that's *whole* life—"caring about other people." There's no one in there trying to be "good" by helping people. The only thing left in the Dalai Lama is the wisdom of compassion. There is no one *doing* good or helping people in order to feel good about himself. Everything he does is motivated by compassion, caring, and lovingkindness. He's not at all concerned with his own personal happiness; he has accomplished that. There's nothing selfish and personal left in him. He is identified with all of us, all of humanity.

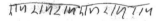

Service and Hanuman

I learned a lot about selfless service from Roshi Bernie Glassman, who is a recognized lineage holder in the Japanese Zen Buddhist tradition. I met Roshi Glassman for the first time at the Sivananda Ashram in the Bahamas. It was love at first sight. I'd heard a lot about the way he takes people on "homeless" retreats on the streets of New York. He and a group of students go and live on the streets for a week or so without money or credit cards. When they want to read a paper, they take it out of the trash; for food, they go to soup kitchens or beg; when they need to sleep, they either bed down in the street or in shelters. I was very intrigued by this—and also scared stiff.

Bernie's wife, who had co-founded the Greyston Foundation, which serves the homeless as well as people living with AIDS, had died shortly before we met, and someone had given Bernie a copy of my CD *Pilgrim Heart* to provide him with some comfort during this time. I didn't know this, but he used to listen to "Namah Shivaya" over and over on his computer as he was writing and working.

When Bernie and I met, we had a powerful connection. He appointed me Music Master of the Zen Peacemakers, a service organization that he created. One day he told me, "We have this

Japanese Buddhist prayer called 'The Gates of Sweet Nectar.'" He gave me the first eight lines and asked, "Do you think you could do something with this?"

"Like what?"

"Well, we Buddhists aren't that good with melody. Maybe you could put a nice melody to this and then all of my students will sing it like that."

"All right, I'll try."

"Good. When we have our annual meeting of the Zen Peacemaker Community, you can sing it there."

Oh, thanks! "When is that?"

"In about 11 months."

"Okay, good." Lots of time, no pressure.

Ten months and two weeks went by . . . I didn't have any melody, and the meeting was coming up. I kept looking at the words, and finally I e-mailed him: "Bernie, can I mess with the words a little? I can't quite get it together."

I received a one-word reply: "Mess." Very Zen. Later on, after I'd finished, he sent me a message that said: "Now you can start to work on the rest of the prayer," which is five pages long.

It took me a year to do eight lines. So I wrote back: "Bernie, it'll take me about three lifetimes to do that."

I got back another one-word response: "Two."

This prayer, "The Gates of Sweet Nectar" (*Kon Ron Mon* in Japanese), is a wholehearted offering to all beings in all forms in all worlds who are hungry, lost, or suffering. We invite them for a meal, which is symbolic of offering them the compassion of our enlightened heart, or the Bodhi Mind. This is how we enter into the Gates of Sweet Nectar. The concept of an offering of compassion is found in all traditions; it is through caring and considering the happiness of other beings that our hearts open.

The Gates of Sweet Nectar
(Krishna Das's version)

Calling out to hungry hearts
Everywhere through endless time
You who wander, you who thirst
I offer you this Bodhi Mind
Calling all you hungry spirits
Everywhere through endless time
Calling out to hungry hearts
All the lost and left behind
Gather round and share this meal
Your joy and your sorrow
I make it mine.

When the melody came to me at last, I realized that it was also a good one for the "Hanuman Chalisa"; I thought the two hymns would complement each other beautifully.

It is said that we're able to make offerings for the sake of others only if we have very good karmas. There are many obstacles to remove first, such as selfishness, greed, and fear. In order to make this offering, we need great strength, and since Hanuman is the embodiment of strength and loving service, as well as the remover of obstacles, we invoke him to help us. Hanuman makes the impossible possible.

We *want* to be kind. We *want* to be helpful. We want to do good and be good human beings, but we're afraid. We don't know how to find the strength to conquer our shortcomings. So we invoke the deepest place in our hearts where Hanuman lives, ✳ which is nothing but strength and wisdom and kindness, and then we can make that offering. By making the offering and reaching out to other beings, we're overcoming our self-centeredness and connecting to a deeper place inside, and by invoking that place in ourselves, our hearts get stronger and more clear. So that's why the prayer and the Chalisa work so well together.

In the story of Ram—the *Ramayana*—Hanuman is not only the perfect servant, but he's also like Superman. There's nothing Hanuman can't do: He's endowed with all virtues. He has all the yogic powers. He's not caught or limited by a sense of separateness. He is the perfect karma yogi. He performs all of his actions in service of the Divine, knowing that God is the doer and that the results of his actions depend on God.

Maharaj-ji said, "Hanuman is the breath of Ram," the breath of God. God is not far away from us but as close as our breath. In his book *The Unvarnished Gospels,* a translation of the four Gospels from the original Greek, Andy Gaus writes that the meaning of the word that was later translated as *spirit,* as in "holy spirit," is actually "breath." The divide between God and man, between holy (as in spirit) and evil (as in body) that characterizes the Western religious teachings is totally absent here. Breath is in the body. Breath is a part of life. It is natural to us. It is concrete. Breath flows in and out of the body and gives us life. We know what it is. Like our breath, God lives within us.

Hanuman is considered to be Ram's greatest devotee because he lives completely with the awareness that Ram, or God, lives in his own heart as who He truly is. He remains separate out of love, only in order to serve. There is no other program running, no personal desires to be fulfilled. Instead of entering and disappearing into Ram, like a drop in the ocean, he keeps a slight separateness in order to serve. He looks back from that oneness toward those who are suffering in the world. He sees the hidden Ram inside of us and serves our hidden divinity by calling to us to come to where he lives, always in the presence of God.

In the *Ramayana,* Ram inquires of Hanuman, "What is your relationship with Me?"

Hanuman answers, "As a body, I am Your servant; as an individual soul, I am a part of You and You are the whole; as the Self, we both are one. This is my firm conviction."

Maharaj-ji after five years in a cave in the town
of Neem Karoli. *(Courtesy of Keshav Das.)*

Maharaj-ji was worshipped as an actual form or manifestation
of Hanuman. Looking at our guru from the outside with normal
human eyes, the other devotees and I saw a sweet little old man
in a blanket throwing fruit in all directions, laughing, patting us
on the head, talking, arranging for the festivals at the temple,
saving lives, healing sickness, giving blessings. But if we could
have looked with the divine eye, we would have seen that he was
immersed in God all the time. The outside stuff *happened,* but he
was fully turned toward that love all the time.

One time in Kainchi, Ram Dass was very upset and walked up
to the takhat where Maharaj-ji was sitting. In those days, we used
to sit on the opposite side of the courtyard and watch Maharaj-
ji from a distance until we were called, so walking up without
having been called was a big deal. He sat down and said, "Maharaj-
ji, I want you to raise my kundalini." Ram Dass was telling him,
"I've had enough. Do it to me. Finish it here and now!"

Maharaj-ji looked at Ram Dass for a moment. Finally, he replied, "I don't know anything about that stuff. You should go see [he named another baba]."

Getting more upset, Ram Dass retorted, "No, Maharaj-ji, *you* raise my kundalini."

"Really, I don't know how to do that. You go see that other baba."

Now Ram Dass was very angry. "*No!*" he shouted. "*You* raise my kundalini!"

Maharaj-ji got up to go inside. He turned and looked down at Ram Dass and said, "I only know two things: *Raa* and *Ma*. [The two syllables of the name of Rama.]" He turned and left Ram Dass sitting there.

> *The world passed away reading big tomes.*
> *None found enlightenment therein.*
> *He who understood the two-and-half letters*
> *which embody love (Ram) gained emancipation.*

— Kabir[23]

Maharaj-ji had told Ram Dass the truth. There was no one inside there to make a decision to do anything for anyone. It was only God, in Whom he was fully merged, Who would and could do what had to be done when the right time came. He was the perfect servant, living in harmony with his Master, Ram/God.

Ramana Maharshi said that realized beings have no *sankalpa*, no personal will of their own. They're surrounded by all of the energy and power of the universe, and because of their total merging with God, whatever has to happen for others will happen through them, without them doing anything. This is a really important point. These great beings aren't sitting around patting themselves on the back for how cool they are. They *are* cool; they're the coolest beings in the universe, but they don't care. They're here to serve; they're here for *us*. They don't hold on to anything—they give it all away. And so it's constantly going through them, full force.

So long as "I" existed in me, the Teacher was not met.
Now the Teacher exists, "I" is gone,
Narrow is the lane of Love, it cannot
contain both the ego and my Lord.

— Kabir[24]

When you understand how to love <u>one</u> thing—then
you also understand how best to love everything.

— Novalis[25]

That's Hanuman. Hanuman has the strength to help us overcome all obstacles so that we can bring ourselves to the feet of that love, into the presence of that love. When we drop our stuff even for a moment and allow that love to flow into and out of us . . . that's Hanuman. We overcome millions of years of depression, millions of years of turning ourselves off, and we finally say, "*Yes. Okay.*" Nothing can close Hanuman's heart. He is the state of total love. The desire and the longing for that love is so strong that nothing can keep him out of it. He knows reality. He knows Ram. He is foremost among gyanis, knowers of the truth. He's in his natural state, which is also our natural state—a state of invocation and dedication where our inner being is falling at the feet of love. That's the real state of our being.

From that place, service is grace.

THE FRUITS OF CHANTING

In 1988 I was sitting in the jungle in India with a very great baba, who looked like he was about 75 but was actually 163 years old. He's even older now! He once asked me, "Do you remember when Lincoln was shot? Oh no, no, no . . . it's okay. We read about it in the papers." He'd done a 12-year course in Ayurveda in Benares, and he said, "It finished sometime in the 1890s." He didn't remember exactly when. It was amazing hanging out with him. He never seemed to do anything—he sat around in this beach chair in the middle of the jungle, relaxed and hanging out. I thought, *This guy's 163 years old . . . what's my hurry? Why am I so tense?*

One day he looked at me—and this was long before I started singing or doing anything in public—and insisted, "You're going to be famous."

I know these yogis can do anything, so I looked up at him and replied, "And rich!"

He chuckled and leaned over really close to me, nose to nose, and very sweetly said, "Famous." Damn!

Another day he looked over at me and simply stated, "You have to develop willpower." I remember thinking: *Willpower? What do I need that for?* He saw what was going on in my head, so he opened me up inside to show me what he was seeing. I saw that I was tripping myself up at every step along the way. I was crippling myself. Day after day after day, I wouldn't fully engage with life. I wouldn't do things with intensity. I was always holding back, not able to jump in and get really involved for so many different reasons: fear of failing or being judged, lack of ability to focus on anything, and just general wimpiness of spirit. I saw that what he meant by willpower was that I needed to develop the strength to live fully and allow the things I wanted and needed to come to me.

This experience made a tremendous impression on me, and I began to change my outlook on things.

Many years earlier, before I'd gone to India, I was staying at The Lama Foundation in New Mexico with Ram Dass, and we heard about a guy named Herman who had been to India and was now living nearby down the mountain. Some people used to go and meditate with him, so we went to see him. Everybody was talking, and I was hanging out in the back, listening. As we were leaving, he turned and pointed at me. "You have to figure out why it is you can't give yourself a hundred percent to whatever it is you're doing," he announced. He nailed me. That was in 1969, and I never forgot it. No matter what I was doing, I saw that I wasn't able to give myself to it; I was always holding back. I didn't want to hold back, but I couldn't help it. So nothing was ever enough. Now I was hearing it again in another way. This time I was in a position to start doing something about it.

Through this ancient baba's eyes, I saw there was *no difference* between the "spiritual" me and the "worldly" me, between spiritual life and worldly life. There was only the life I was living. When we're hungry, how does food get to our mouths? We use our will to raise our arm up and eat. When we want to talk to somebody, we have to move our mouth—that's willpower. Everything we want and need we get through the exercise of our will. It's not enough to want something; we have to be able to act in order to realize that desire. In life, we have to create the circumstances where our desires can come to us. Today I'm using the same willpower to sit down and sing with people—to really give myself to the practice—as I use to get through the day. I had an unconscious belief that I shouldn't have the things I wanted. I had a hidden belief that living in the world was not as "holy" as being a renunciant. In reality, the only thing I had to learn was how to renounce my self-hatred. If I didn't have the strength to go after the things I needed and wanted in my daily life, then how would I find real love/God?

It takes an *extraordinary* amount of willpower and courage to be honest with ourselves, to be honest with another person, to open ourselves up. It takes tremendous strength to allow ourselves to be vulnerable. We say we want a good relationship, but how can that happen if in our unworthiness we don't let it happen? I didn't know where the strength would come from. *I* didn't have it. I was afraid of everything. And so *nothing was happening* in my life. This baba saw all of this, and when he showed me—and I saw it—everything began to change.

These spiritual window-shoppers,
who idly ask, "How much is that?" Oh, I'm just looking.
They handle a hundred items and put them down,
shadows with no capital.

What is spent is love and two eyes wet with weeping.
But these walk into a shop,
and their whole lives pass suddenly in that moment,
in that shop.

Where did you go? "Nowhere."
What did you have to eat? "Nothing much."

Even if you don't know what you want,
buy something, to be part of the exchanging flow.

Start a huge, foolish project,
like Noah.

It makes absolutely no difference
what people think of you.

— Rumi[26]

Nowadays I'm constantly traveling around the world to chant with people, so again and again I'm given the opportunity for intense practice . . . even when I don't feel like it. When I'm sitting in front of a group of people, I have to be really present. Because of this, I've developed the ability to zero in and allow stuff to fall away. It takes a lot of will, effort, wisdom, and intention to reach that moment when we can sit down to sing. Everything about that is positive. It shows a desire to free ourselves. And as time goes on, this ability gets stronger.

One of the results of chanting over a long period of time is that we begin to experience the freedom that comes from within. We begin to see that we've been projecting our movie—the movie of Me—onto the screen of the so-called outside world. As the lens on the projector gets freer of dust, what we see on the outside changes. Eventually we recognize that if we could clean the dust off that lens completely, then the fear, selfishness, greed, anger, and shame would disappear, and our light would shine out completely and radiantly.

The sun rises, and its light shows us what the world looks like. We see the world more clearly as the light shines more brightly. The higher the sun rises, the clearer the landscape becomes, and we're able to find our way more easily. Before the sunrise, we had no doubt that we were seeing the world clearly, and we lived and moved according to what we saw. But as the light increases, we realize that we weren't seeing things as they truly are. Guru/God/ Self is that light . . . always shining on us. The practice of the Name turns us in the direction of the light. The practice of the Name removes the dust from our eyes so that we can see the world as it really is: lit up by the light of the guru.

As time goes on, the gravity of this planet of "me" loses its strength, and our stuff flows away into space. We don't necessarily notice as it's happening; if we look at our lives over time, however, we might see that the quality of our days is lighter and we're getting more of the things we need and want. We might also have the feeling that getting through the day is not as hard as it used to be.

I know I don't mope around as much as I used to. I was a great moper. I miss it. Now when I mope, I really enjoy watching myself. *Look at him. He's moping around the house. How amazing! Jeez, he's really caught in it. Unbelievable!* I also don't watch sports as much as I used to. I don't know where the guy went who used to grab some chips and guacamole on Sundays and gap out for ten hours on football. I don't remember seeing him move his stuff out of the house, but he's gone. I still put the TV on, but the next thing I know, I'll be doing something else in another room. The need to disappear in unconsciousness for so long is just gone.

I guess that's the whole point of practice. I feel like I'm the same jerk I always was, with the same issues nagging me to death, *but* I don't think about myself as much as I used to. The amount of time spent in those heavier states of mind with the same old boring self-judgmental stuff is much less than it used to be. The thing is that we don't get to pat ourselves on the back for it. We might not even notice, but through practice, over time, the heaviness goes away. I don't know about you, but I'll take that any day.

I've noticed that one of the fruits of my practice is a growing ability to be aware of reactions and feelings as they arise in me. I'm able to see that many of my feelings and judgments are programs that have been running for a long time. It seems that nowadays there's more space around these programmed reactions, allowing me to question whether they're as real as I used to believe they were. The tricky thing about states of mind, including so-called higher experiences, is that when we're in them, they feel total and permanent—and then we're not in them anymore. Heaven is a state of mind, the quality of which is "eternal happiness." As long as it lasts. Eternal damnation is eternal when we're in it. Then, of course, we get a phone call from somebody who says "I love you," and that changes our whole head around and that's the end of eternal damnation.

Once I was driving down to New York to deliver some of my CDs to a radio station. I put them on the seat of the car and thought, *Everyone else listens to me in their car, why don't I?* So I put one in and was happily singing along, *Hare Krishna Hare Krishna,* when a car cut in front me, almost causing an accident. I went from heaven to hell in a split second. "Son of a bitch!" I screamed, and I immediately sped up so that I could take a good look at who had cut me off. To my embarrassment, it was a little old lady, barely able to see over the steering wheel, who was struggling to stay on the road. I hadn't been the target of someone's malevolent action—I didn't even exist to her. She was navigating through her world as best she could, as I was navigating through mine, but I'd interpreted her actions in a certain way based on my programming.

The longer I sing, the more I'm freed from my programming. Over time, as the chanting has gotten deeper, it's affected my day-to-day life. I notice that I spend less time living unconsciously. When I sing, I'm pulled out of my thinking into the inner-directed flow of the chant, away from the front lines of total engagement with my sensors firing around me. Through the repetition of the Name, I'm training my mind to release itself from involvement in those programs. Over time, I've seen those programs slow down and become more transparent.

The simple fact that we begin to notice these thoughts and feelings as they arise is a fruit of practice. We have a brief moment to let go before that wave of emotion comes over us and renders us helpless. We can't stop a reaction through reasoning or will, but when we move more deeply into ourselves through practice, the gap between our perceptions and reactions grows and allows us to notice what is going on inside ourselves before we get totally wiped out. We may not be able to stop the reaction, but the noticing makes it softer and easier to let go. Maybe the wave only goes up to our knees instead of 50 feet over our heads. The emotions still might wash over us, but they recede more quickly, and we see them for what they are before we act on them and create even more drama. That spaciousness is the natural result of practice.

Practice isn't only while we're sitting down chanting. It begins like that, but gradually we're digging down to a deeper place in our own hearts that we live in. If we close down, it becomes more obvious to us than it was before. It hurts more. A boat that's out on the ocean and doesn't want to get tossed around by the waves has to drop an anchor down. By doing our practice, we're sinking the anchor deeper into the ocean of the Name. We're developing a deeper center of gravity that allows us to more easily let go of disturbing experiences. We need leverage. Practice gives us that.

What I've discovered from doing so much chanting and practices of different kinds over the years is an unknown muscle located somewhere deep in my heart. It's the "letting go" muscle. After many years, I realized that I've been unknowingly exercising this hidden muscle. It's been getting stronger as time goes on and has now developed the ability to automatically kick in whenever I'm bombarded by negative thoughts or caught in my habitual obsessive patterns. As soon as I reach a certain level of self-torture, the muscle flexes and allows me to let go, and I can bring my attention to the sound of the Name being sung inside me. As soon as I hear the Name, I begin to sing along, and slowly the ironlike grip of those old thought-forms begins to relax. Back again!

Practice helps us find that place inside, over and over again, and gives us faith in ourselves—the confidence that we can sit down and *do* this. In fact, our entire lives begin to revolve around finding this inner sense of well-being. In the meantime, when the hard stuff happens, we deal with it as best we can. The more practice we do, the easier it is to recognize the cycle: we go under, we come up, we go under, we come up. We always come up. Sometimes I wake up and go, "Wow, I've got a hell of a day ahead of me." Then I tell myself, "Wait a minute. All I have to do is sing!" I don't have to have everything figured out in advance. *I don't have to be so involved in my own story line.* I can let the mantra of the Name flow on and let my life do whatever it does.

Once when I was on tour, somebody had stolen my laundry from the hotel washing machine. I was pissed. I had to leave for the kirtan without having found my favorite red T-shirt. But then I sat down and began to sing, and life immediately got very simple. *All I had to do was sing.* It was very liberating. I didn't have to do anything else at that moment except sing and allow the Name to draw me within. How fantastic! And when I got back to the hotel, my laundry was back.

All I have to do is sing.

SINGING FOR MY LIFE

In the '80s, I started a record company that at first was dedicated to helping the older generation of jazz masters make new recordings of their music. As time went on, I was drawn more to world music and began to record and produce music from many different cultures around the world. Later on, having a record company came in very handy when I wanted to make a chanting CD. At the time, there was no other company that would have released it!

In 1994, after realizing that I had to chant with people, it was still difficult to do it. In the beginning, I was happy chanting at Jivamukti. Whenever I was in New York on a Monday, I went there and sang with whoever showed up, usually a group of about 10 or 15 people. I used my *ektar,* a one-stringed drone instrument, but after a while it wasn't loud enough for a group, so I started to play the harmonium. I'd taken piano lessons as a kid, so I was able to figure out the chants well enough to play along as I sang.

After a few months, I began to feel a vague uneasiness. More people were starting to be attracted to the chanting, but I couldn't miss seeing that they were becoming interested in me as well. And I was enjoying the attention. It was fun, yet at the same time I realized that I was getting caught up in it. I began to fear that I might start singing from the wrong place. The feeling of unease grew into a feeling of disgust with myself for getting so easily caught in my desires. I was a hungry guy, and I knew that sooner or later I'd start gobbling up everything in sight and create a hell world for myself and everyone else as well.

A deep despair began to grow inside of me. Chanting was the only thing I could do to help myself, and I was scared that I'd be unable to stop myself from using the situation to feed my own desires. If I couldn't do it in a good way—as an offering to my guru, as a way to reconnect with that love again—then I didn't want to do it at all. It would simply turn into a way of getting attention and fame. As Ramana Maharshi once noted, when you ask the thief to be the policeman, a lot of investigation will go on, but no arrest will ever be made.

In March of 1995, I finally reached the end of my rope. I left for India and vowed that I'd never chant with people again unless Maharaj-ji fixed what was wrong in my heart. I had no idea what this meant, but I knew something had to change inside me, and I knew that only he could do it.

I arrived in India and went to stay with the Tewaris in Lucknow. K.C. was my best friend and teacher, and I was going to lay it all out to him. He'd never failed to help me find a way out of my problems. But when I arrived in Lucknow, I found that everything had changed. The family was in an unhappy state. Ma was very sick, and Baba would lie in bed all day with his eyes closed, not moving and hardly ever talking. I'd sit next to him on a chair for hours at a time in silence. Then when I'd get up (for instance, to go to the bathroom), he'd jump up and ask with great anxiety, "Where are you going?"

"Baba, just to the bathroom."

"You'll come back?"

"Yes, right away."

"Okay." Then he'd lie down again and disappear into silence.

This went on for weeks. I couldn't understand what was going on, and my despair deepened as I realized that no help was going to come from him. I had nowhere else to turn. I was left on my own with my problem.

It was getting hot in Lucknow. I can't stand the heat, so we planned to go up to the Tewaris' house in the hills where it would be cooler. Unfortunately, Ma was too sick to travel. Instead, I took her to the doctor almost every day for tests, going by rickshaw in the brutal heat of the midday sun. Mad dogs and Englishmen, indeed! None of the doctors could understand why her blood pressure was so high and none of her medications seemed to be working. Then one day she tearfully admitted that she hadn't been taking the pills at all. It turns out that earlier that winter, K.C. had gone to the Sangam in Allahabad to take a sacred bath. It was very cold and he came down with pneumonia. Thinking that he was going to die, Ma stopped taking her blood-pressure medicine. As a good Indian wife, she wanted to die before her husband. Yet even when he recovered, she didn't start taking it again.

She began taking her pills again, and after a week or so her blood pressure came down. We were finally able to leave for the hills with Sharad, the Tewaris' eldest son. A few weeks later, Sri Siddhi Ma came back to Kainchi, which was less than an hour away, and we all visited. Siddhi Ma told me that I could come to stay at Kainchi when Neelu, the Tewaris' second son, came with his wife to take care of K.C. and Ma. Siddhi Ma asked what my plans were. I told her that I had to be back in New York by the end of May, which was in about three weeks. She was quiet for a minute and then replied, "No, you have to stay until June 15th," the annual *bhandara* celebration of the consecration of the Hanuman temple in Kainchi. Then she added, "You have to see Maharaj-ji's big form."

I thought that was a really strange thing to say. I had no idea what she meant by it, but she'd pushed one of my big buttons.

In 1972, when I'd gotten sick at Kainchi, Maharaj-ji had sent me to the hospital in Nainital. Because of that, I'd missed the June 15th bhandara at the temple. On that day, Maharaj-ji had worn a red plaid blanket. It was the only time in all my years with him in India that he'd worn red, which is Hanuman's color, and I was very upset that I missed seeing him in it. After he left his body, I vowed that I would never attend another bhandara on that day at Kainchi. In fact, more than once over the years I'd left Kainchi just before the bhandara, only to return after the 15th. I was uneasy about breaking my vow, but if Ma was asking me to stay, I thought I should. I made some phone calls back to the U.S. to see if I was needed. I wasn't, so when I went back to Kainchi, I reluctantly told Ma that I could stay.

A week later I moved into the temple. I was so happy to be there. I started singing with the kirtan walas for many hours every day. It was a dream come true to be able to chant like this hour after hour and let my cares and worries fly away. Nevertheless, I had a problem that kept gnawing at me.

I found a spot at the back of the temple where I could watch the night sky. I'd look up at the stars, and all I could see was my own sorrow. I felt so separate from Maharaj-ji that it was almost unbearable. I said to him, "Maharaj-ji, if you send me back to the U.S. like this, without your blessings, I can't be responsible for my actions!"

I swear I heard him laughing . . . but nothing happened.

One day Siddhi Ma called me over. I told her that I felt like I'd never gotten over not coming back to see Maharaj-ji before he left his body. She talked to me for a while and then sent me away. I thought that I'd offended her somehow by my lack of faith. And then I had a powerful dream that night: I was waiting to go into a dentist's office when my teeth suddenly began to fall out, and I was choking on them. Just at that moment, the doors to the office burst open and Siddhi Ma came in wearing a dentist's uniform. She started pulling the teeth out of my mouth and saved me from choking to death. I woke up in a sweat. When I told Tewari the dream, he said, "Great! She's removing the obstacles in your way."

There were only a few days left before the bhandara, and then I'd have to return to America. Nothing had changed in my heart; I knew that. I was in great despair. To be prevented by my own stuff from doing the only thing that could help me get rid of that very "stuff" was horrible.

The night before the bhandara, I went out in the dark behind the temple, looked up to the sky, and called out to Maharaj-ji, "You haven't done anything yet. This is your problem. I'm singing to people in your name. Do something!"

In the old days, Maharaj-ji had told me to wear a long red ulfie, which I did while I lived in India. I'd brought my old ulfie with me on this trip, but I vowed to myself that I wouldn't wear it unless somehow Maharaj-ji or Siddhi Ma told me to put it on again. Every time I met Ma on that trip, she'd introduce me to the devotees like this: "This is Krishna Das. He was the first priest of the Durga temple. He used to wear a long red ulfie." I'd wait for her to ask, "Why don't you wear it now?" But she never did. So I didn't. Since it was very hot in Kainchi at this time, I wore a light T-shirt and a lightweight *lungi* (long piece of cloth wrapped around the waist).

The morning of the bhandara, which is a special day for Hanuman, I came out of my room on the way to chant . . . and I stopped. I said to myself, *Krishna Das, you are such a jerk. You're still trying to bribe Maharaj-ji! You know you want to wear the red ulfie; just do it. You don't need anyone to tell you anything. Maharaj-ji himself asked you to wear it and he liked it, so put it on.* I went back to the room and changed my clothes.

When I came out, the people who were there for the bhandara all stared at me. I could see them wondering, *Who is this big white monkey in a red ulfie?* But I just went down and sang with the kirtan guys. Listening to my heart like that, I'd taken a small but very necessary first step toward being freed from my difficult situation. I didn't realize it, but I'd entered the river that would lead me into the ocean of love. I sang for a couple of hours. Then I rested, and when I woke up I took a bath.

There were thousands of people in the temple, and tens of thousands more lining up on the road outside, all waiting to take their prasad. Siddhi Ma had come to the back of the temple and was sitting on the ledge by the steps, meeting people as they were leaving after taking prasad. I went and stood near her, and for a long time, I just looked out over the whole scene. From where I stood, I could see the line of devotees all the way out to the road and beyond, slowly moving along. I saw the devotees who were busy serving and the commotion on all sides.

As I looked out over the scene, it seemed to me that Maharaj-ji was in total control of every action, every thought, of each and every person there. I saw that he had pulled all of these people to Kainchi, was putting the food in their mouths, and then was leading them back to where they came from. The funny thing was that I also saw that they all thought *they* had brought themselves there! *Why don't we go to that bhandara in Kainchi? We can take that train and this bus, have our prasad, and return by the next day. . . .*

The mysterious ways of the great masters are not visible to us. Maharaj-ji seemed to be doing nothing, but it was all happening as it should just the same. He was taking care of everything—from cutting vegetables to making sure the sun rose and set perfectly. Although these were more like thoughts than true visions, I was feeling very peaceful and relaxed nonetheless.

That night I went to the back of the ashram again and looked out at the stars. I said to Maharaj-ji, "Well, it looks like you're not going to do anything to fix me. I have to leave in a few days, and nothing has changed yet. I guess that's the way it's going to be, and it's okay. What can I do? I know that I can't make you do anything you don't want to do. I'll go back to America like this. It's not so bad; I can get along. I'll sing kirtan, and I'll deal with it. Somehow everything will be all right." Then, as I turned to go back to the room, a huge shooting star burst through the sky! I felt like Maharaj-ji was saying, "Okay. It's a deal."

Now I'd been cut loose from the river bank, and I was flowing freely toward the ocean. Of course, I still had no idea of what was to come.

ᚠᚢ ᛚᚠᚨᛋᛗᚱᛚᚠᛋ ᛚᚠᛏᚠᚢ

When I woke up the next morning, I gradually realized that I was feeling a deep peace, which for me was very unusual. Maharaj-ji had begun to lift me into himself so gently that I hadn't even noticed. I was floating calmly in a deep, relaxed space, feeling very much at ease and very quiet inside.

On the afternoon of June 17th, I was waiting to see Siddhi Ma before leaving Kainchi. I realized that in all the time I'd been there, I hadn't spent any time at the Durga temple where I'd once been the pujari.

There were still a lot of people around, so I went behind the temple and sat down where I wouldn't be disturbed. I leaned my back against the wall of the temple, closed my eyes, and immediately felt a lightness of being. When I opened my eyes, I realized that I'd been "gone" for a long time. As I came back to consciousness, "I" was no longer around in the same way. There was only vast Presence, full and empty at the same time—a vast space in which everything was held, outside of which there could be nothing. Far off in this space, it seemed as if there was a slight thickening of the atmosphere, a small cloud of thoughts. When I noticed it, I realized, *Oh, that's Krishna Das-ness.* I saw that "me," those thoughts, were not who I am, even when I was thinking them! The thought *So who am I?* didn't arise, because there was no one to have the thought. There was just deep peace and being.

Everyone I saw was filled with beauty and love, and there was no distance between us. There was no hurry. There was all the time in the world to be there and feel this love for everyone. It wasn't "my" love, and it wasn't Maharaj-ji's love. He was not different from this Presence that surrounded everything and everyone. The whole world was filled by this vast Presence and deep sweetness. It was all happening in him. There was nothing outside of this, nor could there be.

Maharaj-ji had breathed me into a place of calm and peace and stillness. He was huge. There was no place that he was not.

He had lifted me into himself, beyond my emotions and any understanding I thought I had about him. The curtain had parted for a moment, and he'd allowed me to experience a small part of himself. The amazing thing was that I hadn't realized that anything was happening to me. He'd thrown his blanket over me and pulled me so close to him that I couldn't see him with the eyes of my emotions and mind. I could only *be* in his presence, enveloping the whole universe.

When I walked across the courtyard, nothing was moving. People were talking and life was going on, but there was only stillness, wrapped up in the deepest, sweetest peace. Everywhere I turned, love was rushing toward me. People were coming to say good-bye, and I was free to embrace them with open arms. I didn't have to push them away or turn away from the love. I was home in him. Ever since the time when I hadn't returned to sing to him before he left his body, there had been a knife in my heart. That knife was gone. I was free of the past and all its heartbreak.

 I saw that "me-ness/Krishna Das-ness" was like a little bubble on the surface of the ocean. When I'm thinking, *I'm Krishna Das*— the bubble—it doesn't mean that the ocean is gone. It just means that I'm not aware of it. What I believed about myself didn't affect this Presence, didn't alter it or change it. This Presence is always here and nothing can exist outside of it. I saw that it was okay to be "stupid" and think I was "me" because, even when I thought I was "me," I wasn't! That's only a temporary insanity. If I think that I'm the wave, does the ocean disappear? The wave is nothing but ocean, taking a fleeting shape due to the winds of karma.

I have been thinking of the difference between water
and the waves on it. Rising,
water's still water, falling back,
it is water, will you give me a hint
how to tell them apart?

Because someone has made up the word
"wave," do I have to distinguish it
from water?

There is a Secret One inside us;
the planets in all the galaxies
pass through his hands like beads.

That is a string of beads one should look at with luminous eyes.

— Kabir[27]

In Kainchi, 1972. *(Courtesy of Chaitanya.)*   In Kainchi, 1995.

I was now free to go back to the West and start singing again, to be able to give myself 100 percent to the chanting. I no longer had to be afraid of messing up. I saw that the people who I thought were attracted to me weren't really attracted to me at all. They wanted connection to *that place,* that place of love that I also wanted to be connected to. It wasn't about me, even when I thought it was! I could breathe, maybe for the first time in this life. The river had reached the ocean; water flowed into water, and there was only water. I got into the car and drove out of the Kainchi valley.

And nothing was moving in the universe.

The taste of this experience stayed with me for almost nine months. For all that time, I could still feel that space, although I noticed that it was fading slowly. One day I realized that it had become a memory. The change it effected was so deep that I have to say it separates my life into "before" and "after." It seemed like some very fundamental way of being in the world changed for me.

When I arrived in New York from India, I went to visit some friends. As I walked into their apartment, they were watching video footage of Maharaj-ji. When I saw him on the TV, I cracked up and said, "That's not Maharaj-ji. That's the Maharaj-ji doll." I understood intuitively that the real Maharaj-ji, that vast compassionate Being, the Eternal Presence, had entered into a doll/body for our sake. As doll/humans with doll eyes, we could only see other dolls. Out of compassion, in order that we might see—and in seeing, believe—he'd taken a "small" form, a fragment of his own true self. As Krishna had given Arjuna divine sight, so had Maharaj-ji opened my eyes for an instant. For one unforgettable instant.

All I can do is shake my head in wonder at his grace.

FOLLOWING IN THE FOOTPRINTS
OF LOVE: MA AND BABA TEWARI

For me, a real manifestation of Maharaj-ji's grace over the years was living with and traveling in the company of my Indian parents, Ma and K.C. Tewari. We made pilgrimages to sacred places all around India. The Indians would marvel to see Ma Tewari, this tiny woman, holding my hand as we navigated up the hill called Hanuman Dhara in Chitrakut, or slowly descending the *ghats* (broad stairways leading down to the water) in Benares for a bath in the Ganges River.

To see Ma smile was an amazing thing. The compassion and sweetness of her nature radiated like the sun breaking through the clouds, and it made my world okay again for a little while. She fed me until I was ready to explode with food that tasted as if it came from heaven. And her love saved me time and time again from the black hole of my weird Western emotions. Once I hadn't been able to get something she needed, and I told her I was really sorry, that I was a bad son. She looked up at me and asked tenderly, "Where could someone get a son like you?"

K.C. was the best friend anyone could have. No matter how messed up and depressed I was, he always rescued me with love and the bottom line. He was a schoolteacher who had risen to be the principal of one of India's most prestigious schools. But that was just the outer garb. He was a hidden yogi who'd been doing meditation and *tapasya* (spiritual austerities) since his childhood. Wherever we traveled, he received the respect of the sadhus and babas.

One particular saint, Swami Gopalanand, who is a yogi himself, told me that K.C. was the greatest yogi he had seen throughout his many years of involvement with sadhus and great saints. He was fully convinced that K.C. had control over the powers of nature.

The story goes that on the morning when the roof of the Hanuman Temple at Bageshwar, a small village in the hills, was to be laid, there was a shortage of workers. The cement was prepared, so if the concrete wasn't laid in time, it would all go to waste. Swami Gopalanand rushed at 8 A.M. to seek the help of K.C.'s son Sharad, who worked in Bageshwar and had enough influence to get workers arranged. Not finding Sharad, Swami-ji narrated his plight to K.C., who laughed. He told Swami-ji, "For God's work you want to seek the help of a mere man who's just in charge of electricity? God will arrange His work Himself." K.C. assured Swami-ji that by 10:30 that morning, at least 50 workers would reach the temple site.

All of a sudden, the whole sky clouded over and it started raining heavily. There was a large government project being constructed near the temple. The workers refused to work in the downpour, so the supervisor had no alternative except to release them. At 10:30, the rain stopped, and all of the workers reached Swami-ji and got the temple roof laid in time.

On the first of my many pilgrimages with the Tewaris, we were staying with Punjabi Bhagavan, a baba who was the head of a big *sewashram* (place devoted to service) in Janaki Kund, on the banks of the Mandakini River that runs through Chitrakut, a very sacred place in India. In the story of the *Ramayana*, Chitrakut is where Ram came with His wife, Sita, and brother Lakshman after being forced to leave His kingdom. They spent 12 years there surrounded by the peace and beauty of the jungles and hills. The whole area is suffused with a rare sweetness, and there are many wandering sadhus and babas who come there to immerse themselves in devotion to Ram. There is chanting and puja going on day and night.

Punjabi Bhagavan told us that many years earlier, there had been a sadhu who did much intense spiritual practice in a cave on a nearby hillside. Even though he'd done this for a long time, no one knew he was there. One day Maharaj-ji came to the area and was sitting on a rock in the river. He sent someone to "bring the sadhu who's in that cave." At first the sadhu didn't want to be disturbed, but eventually he came to see who had called him. Maharaj-ji was very sweet to the sadhu and inquired about his spiritual practice. Then he told the sadhu that he should leave his practice and build a big ashram there to serve the wandering sadhus. The sadhu refused and went back to his cave to continue his practice. Punjabi Bhagavan then admitted that *he* had been that very sadhu. In the sweetest voice, he said, "If I would have listened to Maharaj-ji that day, all the responsibility for this ashram would be his! But I was young and stubborn. Now here I am doing what he asked me to do, but the whole weight is on my shoulders!"

ॐ नमो भगवते वासुदेवाय

During our time in Chitrakut, I'd been feeling very sad because Siddhi Ma had promised to take me there, but at the last minute she was unable to go. She sent me off with the Tewaris and told me that I'd see Maharaj-ji in Chitrakut. I'd been walking around in the jungles every day, saying out loud, "I'm here, where are you?" Nothing happened, and I was getting depressed. Then I had this powerful dream about Maharaj-ji.

I was in some devotee's house with Maharaj-ji, and we were trying to get out of there so that we could run away from everyone. We ran upstairs and down a hall, but the only way out proved to be a window that was on the second story of the house. Maharaj-ji hopped up to the windowsill and jumped down to the ground below. He landed on his feet and looked up at me as if to say, "Okay, now what are *you* gonna do?" I got up on the windowsill and jumped down as well, doing a somersault and landing right next to him. I looked at him like, "So *there!*" Then we both ran away, laughing hysterically.

In the next scene of the dream, he was sitting in the jungle, surrounded by devotees. He'd point toward the devotees and then at the ground in front of them, and they'd reach down into the ground and bring up jewels and diamonds. I was standing at the back of the group, and he looked at me and pointed to the ground in front of me. I reached down into it and came out with a huge diamond as big as a football. He looked at me again, seeming to ask, "Now what will you do?" I threw the diamond high up into the air and, while all of the other devotees ran to get it, Maharaj-ji and I ran away into the jungle together, arm in arm, laughing wildly with love and joy. It was the most amazing feeling of intimacy and love. Yet it was also a powerful realization—it showed me that, even in my unconsciousness, I wanted *him* more than anything that he could "give."

One day K.C. and I went down to the banks of the Mandakini River and sat on the rock where Maharaj-ji used to sit when he came to Chitrakut. He told me a story about one of Maharaj-ji's devotees, whose son was an unusual kind of drunkard. He and his friends used alcohol as "lubrication" for the heart; they'd sing devotional songs to God all night, then sleep all day. This man, whom we'll call BG, wanted to protect his mother from supposed "holy" men who took money from naïve devotees. When BG heard that Maharaj-ji had been in his house, he vowed that he'd beat the hell out of Maharaj-ji if he ever came again. When Maharaj-ji left the house after another visit, BG leapt up from his sleep and rushed out into the street after him, taking off his shoe so that he could beat Maharaj-ji with it. Devotees tried to stop BG, but Maharaj-ji said, "*No!* Let him come and do what he has to do."

As BG reached Maharaj-ji, he suddenly fell to the ground at his feet and sobbed uncontrollably. At that moment his life totally changed. BG never took another drink.

After this, BG and Maharaj-ji forged a rare and special relationship. They roamed the mountains and jungles of India together. If anyone wanted to know where Maharaj-ji was, all they had to do was find out where BG was because they were always together. Telephones were rare in those days, so it could be very difficult to find Maharaj-ji, who was always wandering from town to town and house to house to visit the devotees. The temples were built only in the last few years of his life to provide a place where devotees could spend more time with him.

Many years passed, and BG's mother died. One day Maharaj-ji told him, "You know those jewels you inherited that are hidden in the drawer of the dresser in the back of the bedroom? Sell them and buy a truck." BG found the jewels, which he hadn't known existed, and bought a big truck. "Okay, buy a load of potatoes and pay x amount for it," Maharaj-ji instructed, "and then take it to this other town and sell it for x amount." Within a short time, BG had a fleet of trucks and was a rich man. Then one day Maharaj-ji said, "You know that land you inherited? Build a little hut and live there like a saint. Don't cut your hair. Wear white clothes." So BG built a little hut and started living there as a sadhu. He sang beautiful devotional songs, and thousands of people were soon going up there to sing with him. He started to have very deep spiritual experiences, and people began respecting him as a saint.

Many ladies also visited, cooking and generally taking care of BG. He became involved with one woman, who got pregnant, and it became a big scandal. Maharaj-ji told him, "Okay, this is finished now. Cut your hair. Close up the cabin. You're married now. Go live with her and raise a family." So he did.

When Tewari finished telling me BG's story, I responded, "Wow, he really blew it, didn't he?"

K.C. looked at me as if I were insane and said, "My boy, is there something wrong with your brain? Don't you realize? This work, this spirituality, is like loading explosives." He explained that Maharaj-ji had brought BG into a very high state of consciousness where his actions created no karma. A human being can only spend a certain amount of time in that state without dropping the body, since there's no use for it anymore. Tewari then added, "Maharaj-ji knew just how many explosives could be loaded before the whole thing would blow up. And this is how he brought BG back into his body: he made him a family man."

One time when K.C. was in his early 30s and single, he and Maharaj-ji visited the house of a devotee in Haldwani who had recently died. The youngest daughter was taking care of the whole family, including her older sisters and their husbands. When Maharaj-ji and Tewari arrived, she served them with much love and respect. She was constantly going in and out of the living room, bringing them things to eat and drink. Maharaj-ji said to Tewari, "Look at her, how beautiful she is. How beautifully she serves." Maharaj-ji kept on talking about her and her wonderful qualities. Finally he said to Tewari, "You should marry this girl."

Tewari retorted, "I will not. You know I have taken a vow not to marry." Tewari's parents had died when he was very young and he'd been raised by an aunt, who'd also died when he was young. He'd sworn to remain a bachelor and avoid family life.

Maharaj-ji protested, "No, no. You should marry her. Isn't she beautiful? See how she serves everyone. She is actually Joan of Arc." Tewari fiercely refused. Maharaj-ji said, "We're not leaving this house until you agree to marry her." A battle began between the two of them.

Finally at the end of three days, Tewari told Maharaj-ji, "Okay, I'll agree to marry her under one condition. If you agree to take responsibility for everything that comes from this marriage and put it in writing, then I'll do it."

Maharaj-ji replied, "What?! I'll never do that. What do you think I am?"

Tewari said, "Great. Then I won't get married."

Finally, Maharaj-ji agreed to Tewari's terms. I've seen the marriage certificate, which reads, "I, Neem Karoli Baba, take full responsibility for all issue from this marriage," and it's signed in gold ink by Maharaj-ji.

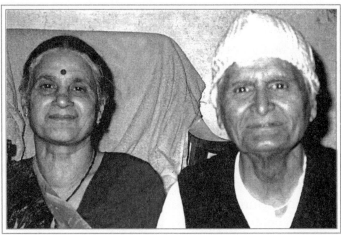

My Indian parents, Ma and K.C. Tewari.

After some time, the day of the marriage arrived. While Tewari was going in the traditional procession to meet the bride, word came that Maharaj-ji was sitting nearby. Tewari left the procession and went to see him. They sat together for a long time until someone asked Maharaj-ji, "What are you doing keeping this guy here? You are holding up the marriage." Maharaj-ji sent Tewari away with words of encouragement, and the marriage was performed.

K.C. had an amazingly earthy sense of humor. Once he was describing all of the fierce yogic practices that he'd done as a young man in order to remain celibate. He described the many hours of *pranayama* (breathing practices) and *asana* (physical poses) he performed daily and told me that he had so much energy he used to take ten ice-cold baths a day to try to control the sexual urge. One day he smiled mischievously at me. "You know, I didn't experience samadhi for the first time until after I was married!" he said with a laugh.

He was a tireless yogi. Every morning he sat up in bed at 4 A.M. and stayed there for hours, lost to the world. When others began to wake and move around the house, he would take the *mala* (prayer beads) that Maharaj-ji had given him and do japa, mantra repetition, throughout the day. There were many mornings when I woke up next to him only to see him sitting there like a living murti of Shiva.

Tewari's idea of a "party" was a long night of puja, ritual prayer. We used to be on the road together and he'd find these little Shiva temples on the side of the road. There would be six inches of water covering the floor with all kinds of stuff crawling around in it. And he'd just get right down in it, sitting there for hours chanting mantras and meditating. I'd be cranky and soaked and trying to avoid getting bit by all of those creepy crawlers! But it was incredible.

Before he met Maharaj-ji, Tewari had another great guru who taught him to chant his pujas, long prayers that go on for hours, at the top of his lungs. Tewari had a voice like a chain saw. So when he did these long pujas on Shivaratri, the big night of worship to Shiva, everyone would hear him. He'd do four Shiva pujas, each taking over three hours, without stopping. Mrs. Tewari would sit there ringing the bell and making the actual offerings. It was fantastic.

One time for Shivaratri, a friend and I went up to where the Tewaris were living on the top of a mountain in Nainital. They started puja about eight at night and finished around six in the morning, and I was determined to stay up for the whole thing. About midnight, my friend lay down and went to sleep. Tewari didn't care, telling me, "You go to sleep right here. Don't go anywhere. You'll still get all the good stuff." But I was determined and stayed up all night. At six in the morning, I woke my friend up, and Tewari came around to give us prasad from the puja.

First he took one apple and gave it to my friend, saying, "I'm giving you the One," meaning the absolute, the Supreme Being. And I looked over, thinking, *Huh? Okay, wow.* Then he came to me and gave me five apples, saying, "I'm giving you the five *tattwas,* the five elements that make up the world." I smiled weakly and said, "Thank you." Inside, I was thinking, *What? You're giving me the world? You give this guy the One? He slept all goddamn night.*

All of the energy from the puja started to hit my brain and I started flipping out. I smiled and thanked him, and my friend and I left to walk back down the mountain, which was so steep that the path went back and forth in switchbacks. You couldn't go straight up or down, so it took about 40 minutes to get back to the hotel. When I got into bed, my thoughts were buzzing so much I felt like I was levitating. *He gave me the world? Why did he give me the world if he gave this guy the One? I was up for hours!* On and on. Totally nuts.

Finally I leapt out of bed and ran straight up the mountain. I was up there in about a minute and a half. I banged on the door, and Tewari opened it with this big smile. He was waiting for me. He knew what he'd done. He said, "Come in, come in. Calm yourself, my boy. Come in." He and Ma gave me tea and some food to eat, and I chilled out.

He was always pushing my buttons and making me crazy in an effort to loosen me up and help me not take myself so seriously. He loved me so much and was always there for me when I was having one of my many meltdowns.

Once I heard a small part of a prayer being sung in a temple, which struck me very deeply. I didn't know what prayer it was, so one night when I was sitting with K.C., drinking chai, I asked him if he'd ever heard a prayer with the words *Narayani Namo Stu Te.*

"Oh yes."

"Will you teach it to me?"

"Of course."

So I got out my notebook, and he began to recite the prayer. At first he started slowly, and I tried to write down the words as I heard them—but after a few minutes, he forgot I was in the room and got immersed in the prayer. I put down my book and sat there, listening. It was a prayer to the Goddess Durga, and he was singing it with very deep emotion. As he reached the end of the prayer, his voice began to choke up and tears started to flow down his cheeks.

Over and over again he repeated, *Narayani Namo Stu Te, Narayani Namo Stu Te.*

Then all of sudden he was quiet. I opened my eyes and saw that he was sitting perfectly still, his arms raised in front of him and tears streaming down his cheeks. I realized that he wasn't breathing. He'd gone into samadhi right before my eyes . . . and it really pissed me off! I couldn't get even a taste of this state of consciousness to save my miserable life, and he couldn't stay out of it long enough to teach me one miserable prayer!

Just then Mrs. Tewari came into the room to get the teacups. I said, "Ma, look at Baba. How long will he be like this?"

Smiling sweetly as she picked up the cups, she simply replied, "Don't know." She went back to the kitchen, leaving me with this crying corpse.

I'd seen real samadhi once before as close up as this, but that was in Maharaj-ji's presence. The thing was that Tewari wasn't even trying to enter into it. It happened naturally because of the purity and strength of his devotion and love. After a while he came back to normal consciousness. He taught me the chant another time.

One time Maharaj-ji and K.C. were in Lucknow. They went down to a little Hanuman temple by the river and Maharaj-ji told him, "Sit down and do your Shiva puja."

Tewari said, "I will not!"

Maharaj-ji insisted, "No. Do your puja, do your puja!"

"I don't care what you say, I'm not going to do my puja."

"Why not?"

K.C. said, "Because I know how you are. You know that once I sit down to do the puja, I've taken a vow not to get up until it is finished, and that will be four hours. The minute I sit down and start, you're going to run away, and I'm going to be here for four hours all by myself."

"No, no, no, I promise I won't. I promise I won't run away."

"Oh, really? Okay, hold your ears [this is the Indian equivalent of cross your heart, hope to die]!"

K.C. made Maharaj-ji hold his ears and promise not to run away. Then he sat down and began his puja. He knew the whole thing by heart. Maharaj-ji sat like a stone in front of him and didn't move for four hours. The second Tewari was finished, Maharaj-ji leapt up and told him, "You miserable guy! How could you keep me here like this? I have so much work to do!" And he ran off.

Another time Tewari came from Nainital to Kainchi Temple and started hollering at Maharaj-ji. "Why did you bring me here? I was happy in Nainital and had no intention of coming here, but you dragged me!"

Maharaj-ji yelled back, "I have nothing to do with it. I drag no one here, but you and I have been together for 83 lifetimes. It just has to happen!" This is the way they played.

On Maharaj-ji's last day at the Kainchi ashram before he left his body, he put Tewari into a very deep samadhi and told him to take care of the Westerners. Maharaj-ji said that he was leaving "central jail" (this world) and that all of the Westerners would bother K.C. from then on. It was a task Tewari had previously avoided. Once, some years before, when Maharaj-ji and K.C. had been alone together, Maharaj-ji reached into his dhoti, pulled out a huge wad of money, and threw it at Tewari. He said that K.C. should go to America and teach meditation.

Tewari started to cry bitterly and asked Maharaj-ji, "Do you think I come here for money?" So Maharaj-ji took the money back. Then Tewari recovered his composure and started teasing Maharaj-ji: "Now I see what kind of baba you are, hoarding money like that! I'm going to tell everyone!"

Maharaj-ji laughed and said, "What money? You think that you're a clever person, but you don't know that I'm the cleverest of all!" He reached into his dhoti again and pulled out a bunch of little pieces of paper. He explained, "I'm getting old and losing my memory, so I keep the names and addresses of the devotees on these scraps of paper. You're a greedy man, so you saw money." The money was gone.

In April 1997, I traveled with Ma and Baba on an overnight train trip from Lucknow to Rishikesh. I helped Ma and Baba get comfortable and tucked in for the night in their lower berths, then I climbed up onto one of the upper ones. By this point, we'd traveled all through India together. I always looked forward to a good sleep on a train, but this night was different. I looked at these two old people and was filled with a joy and happiness that was so intense that I fought sleep for many hours so I wouldn't lose the feeling. There was no place in the universe I would rather have been than on that train with these wonderful beings, traveling from anywhere to anywhere. I felt so blessed, complete and full. It was the last time we traveled together.

I returned to America at the end of April. In August, I spoke to K.C. while he was in the hospital in New Delhi, having just had surgery on his liver. I asked if I should come to be with him, but he told me not to come at that time. He was going to his daughter Minoo's house in Delhi to recover.

At his daughter's house, he recovered completely and was feeling healthier than he had in many years. His eldest son, Sharad, came to visit from Lucknow. After Sharad arrived, he received a phone call from home saying that his son, Nitin, had fallen from the roof of the house and was dead. Tewari said, "He's not dead." Sharad left immediately for Lucknow to find that, in fact, Nitin was not dead, but in a coma. He reported this to his father. Tewari picked up his prayer beads and said, "He [Maharaj-ji] listens to me when I do this," and began to do his prayers. After three days, Nitin came out of the coma and miraculously began to recover.

One day shortly after Nitin had stabilized, Tewari got up early in the morning as usual. He asked Ma what time it was. She said 3:30. He got out of bed and walked to the door of the bathroom. He stopped and stood absolutely still. Ma asked him what was wrong. He didn't reply. He then fell stiffly, banging his head on the wall. He was taken to the hospital and was in a coma for three days, the same amount of time that Nitin had been unconscious, after which he opened his eyes. Minoo, who was sitting with him, asked him how he was. He said, "Perfectly all right," and then he died. He had traded his life for his grandson's.

All during this time, the hospital staff had prevented Ma from seeing Baba for some reason. She was totally distraught when she was told that he had left his body and cried out, "I could have saved him with my mantra!" When Ma did puja with this mantra, the ghee lamps that usually only burned for half an hour or so would stay lit for as long as she sat there doing her prayers, and sometimes all through the night.

I'd just led a kirtan in the Bay Area, the first I'd ever done outside of New York. I was in the airport, on my way to chant in Los Angeles, when I got a call telling me that Tewari had died. I was devastated. I realized at that moment that he'd told me not to come because his love and attachment for me would have made it more difficult for him to leave. He was my best friend. I'd depended on him for everything since Maharaj-ji had died, and now he was gone. The pain of his loss was unbearable.

I returned to India a few months later and spent time with Ma. Seeing me so distraught, she gave me K.C.'s prayer beads—the ones Maharaj-ji had given to him and that he'd used throughout his life for his prayers. Holding those beads, I finally felt some peace in my heart.

Ma had always told Baba that she wanted to die first, as Hindu wives traditionally prefer to die before their husbands. Baba replied, "Well, no matter which one of us goes first, not more than 18 months will separate us." Ma left her body exactly 18 months to the day after Baba left his. Ma's physical suffering had been intense for many years. It was a blessing that she'd been released from the prison of pain that was her body.

Once when she was writhing in agony from neuropathy caused by diabetes, I asked, "Ma, are you all right? Can I do anything?"

She smiled weakly and said, "Don't worry. Machine broken; inside okay."

There are no words to describe the beauty and love that these extraordinary beings embodied. They were in the world, but at the same time, they were completely in God.

Devotion is a disease we catch from those who are already infected with it. From Sri Siddhi Ma, Dada, K.K. Sah, the Tewaris, and many of the other old Indian devotees of Maharaj-ji, I was exposed to this wonderful "illness." I pray that it is terminal.

With Ram Dass, 2008. *(Courtesy of Rameshwar Das.)*

PLANTING SEEDS

*T*here's a beautiful line that Ram Dass used to quote all the time from a book called *Mount Analogue* by René Daumal. It's about how the rooster thinks its crowing brings the sun. The baby thinks its crying brings the mother. But sun and mother both have their own place in the universe, and they do what they do based on their own nature. Tewari used to say to me all the time, "The moment you think you're doing it, the whole game is spoiled."

We tend to think that we alone are responsible for our progress on the path. When we feel responsible for our opening—responsible for making everything happen—the tightness, heaviness, and weight that's placed on our shoulders makes any kind of opening very difficult.

A farmer plants a seed, waters it when needed, and goes away to let it grow. He doesn't stand around waiting for it to sprout. He doesn't try to pull it out of the ground before it's ready. Maharaj-ji planted seeds in us, which I'm sure haven't all sprouted yet.

One chilly day in February 1972, I was sitting with another Western devotee in front of Maharaj-ji. My gurubhai had been reading the Ashtavakra Gita, a book of great wisdom, the sayings of an ancient enlightened saint. Maharaj-ji noticed the book and asked my friend what he'd learned from it. He answered, "Everything is the soul." Maharaj-ji was very happy with this answer and told the few Indian devotees who were sitting there, "He understands. These boys understand everything. They are my disciples." He then reached over and casually placed some ash from the charcoal brazier in our mouths and on our heads, mimicking a formal initiation that normally would have been done with the ash from a sacred fire.

Twelve years later, during a very dark and depressed period of my life, I happened to pick up my old India journal and opened to the page with this story on it. I literally fell on the ground crying. How could I have forgotten? It was a gift—a seed that had been planted a dozen years earlier that came to fruition in my heart at the time it was most needed.

Everything we do plants seeds. Every action—even every thought—is a seed that sooner or later will bring some kind of fruit. If we act out of fear and sadness, anger and greed, then those are the seeds we are planting. We don't have to live in fear. The laws of karma are not a prison, they are the key to freedom. We have a choice about what we plant. *We* are planting the seeds, and *we* will reap the fruits. When we understand that what we do *now* has a tremendous effect not only on the rest of our day but the rest of our life, we can exercise some choice about how we greet every moment as it arises.

The planting of seeds is an interesting way of looking at karma. For example, it's said that people who have money now were once very generous in a previous life. But many people with money cling to it tightly and live in fear of losing their wealth. They're not being generous, so they're exhausting the karma that brought them wealth—and planting seeds of future poverty for themselves. That's a simplification, but in essence it is accurate.

With chanting, each repetition of a revealed name of God plants a seed. As Sri Ramakrishna once explained:

> Each and every revealed Name of the One Reality possesses irresistibly sanctifying power. Even if the energy of the Divine Name does not produce immediate results, its repetition will eventually be fruitful—like a seed fallen on the roof of a deserted house which crumbles over decades, finally enabling the germinated seed to take root. The conventional world and the conventional self are this disintegrating old structure.[28]

Each and every repetition of the Name is like a seed that gets caught up by the wind and comes to rest on the roof of an old house. Then, over the course of time and with the passage of seasons, the conditions become good for the seeds to take root. They grow and grow until finally they destroy the roof of the house. They keep growing and go on to crumble the walls and windows and doors. Ramakrishna says that this old house—our sense of me-ness, the conventional self, our separateness—is destroyed. While the house was still standing, there was inside and outside, me and others. When all of the walls are gone, however, there is no "me"—only the great One, the atman.

This is an amazing teaching. Based on his own experience, Ramakrishna is telling us that every repetition of the Name *will* be fruitful. There is no doubt about it. When a saint like Sri Ramakrishna tells us that "every repetition of the Divine Name must have an effect," we have to take his word for it, but our faith is based on an understanding of the greatness of the being who said it. We recognize that he has found what we're looking for and is simply telling us where to look and how to get there. This gives us enough faith or confidence to sit down and do the practice.

One thing Ramakrishna doesn't dwell on is how we feel during this process. Do we feel high? Do we have visions? Do we feel spiritual? It doesn't matter, because it's not about what we feel. *We* are what is being dissolved. It's not about *me and mine.*

Ramakrishna said, "The ego is like a stick dividing water in two. It creates the impression that you are one and I am another." That stick gets removed by the repetition of the Name.

Repeating the Name plants seeds of real *goodness*—seeds that can only grow into the sweet fruit of love, love for ourselves and love for others. Most of us are trying to become good human beings, people who don't want to hurt ourselves or others, but we're often unconscious slaves to the habits we've formed in our lives. It takes time to transform the destructive, hurtful, angry, fearful, and greed-based actions that we perform unconsciously every day.

If you grew up in New York, as I did, you may have about eight feet of armor around you and think that's normal. Most of us walk down the street with the attitude, *Nobody's going to mess with me.* We don't tend to look at each other either. But if we want to be happy, how can we continue to shield ourselves in fear and anxiety? We have to ease that hurt in ourselves. If we want to be happy, if we want love, if we want caring, if we want kindness in our lives, then it's very simple: to have more kindness, all we have to do is start being kind. Then there's immediately more kindness in the world. People respond to us in a different way. As we get stronger in love, we begin to see that other people are hurting, too. We can plant seeds that will develop into new patterns of activity—actions that aren't so isolating and fear based, actions that will create a wider sense of community in our lives.

Through the continual repetition of these Names, the Presence that lives within us—the presence that lives within our own hearts, our own true nature—reveals itself. We become aware of it through practice. It's as if we're doing this practice while we're asleep and dreaming that we're awake. If we keep chanting, the repetition of the Names will wake us up and show us our own beauty. We don't *know* what it will be like when we do wake up, but we're drawn to the "awake" state like moths to the flame. So we do the practice. And *gradually but inevitably,* we wake up; we open our inner vision and find that place inside ourselves. And that's the whole point.

There's no downside to chanting because, no matter why we do it, it plants a seed every time. Every time we do kirtan or any spiritual practice, we're planting seeds that will help us do *more* of these kind of things. A poster for some teacher who can help us might float through the wind and hit us in the head. Who's to say that it's not because we did this chanting? We don't know. Chanting feeds that place that wants to find a deeper way to connect. We notice how disconnected we are, so we stop doing the things that give us a hangover for three days. Sometimes it seems to me like this whole life is one long hangover, and chanting is the cosmic Alka-Seltzer.

They say that everything that's happening now is the result of things that have happened in the past. The waves we're experiencing now have come to us across the huge ocean of time. We're not totally at the mercy of these waves. Because of the grace of our teachers, we find ways to stabilize the boat of our life. So right now, if I plant a seed of the Name, a seed of turning within instead of a seed of unconscious reacting, I'm changing what will grow. Even one little *Sitaram* is a moment when we're not blindly reacting to the past. So we're creating space and planting seeds that will grow into moments that won't be reactive in the so-called future. The future is now, later.

When we truly understand that the laws of karma are not blind fate, we start to plant seeds that will help us wake up and create the qualities we want to develop. We plant righteous, wholesome seeds of what we want to have in our lives. Less and less, we engage in behaviors that are destructive for us. We're chanting the names of God, of Love, and gradually but inevitably, our lives are transformed. We're chanting the names of this place that lives within us. We're helping each other move inside, to experience our true home.

The light inside, the love inside of us, is always present. It can't be anywhere else. God lives inside of us as *who we really are*. Not as *"God": Some Other Thing*. As *who we are*. Not somebody else. Not something else. Not somewhere else. The feeling of being—of just *being*—that we have within us, the sense of "I," is like the mist coming off the ocean of pure absolute Being. When we're driving to the ocean, we can still be far away, but we get the taste of the ocean air before we reach the water. The Name is like that mist. It carries the wetness of the ocean. Our thoughts and emotions will be purified, get lighter, as we turn toward the Name, just like clouds that are covering the blue sky change and evaporate in the vastness of the sky's spaciousness. We follow this sense of "being" into the ocean of pure awareness, our true Being.

Chanting keeps me straight. It keeps me going back into that deep place inside. It doesn't matter how many people come to chant with me, it's all the same. Everywhere I go, family shows up. We sing, and we get to help each other find that place inside that feels right.

My favorite experience with Maharaj-ji was when I'd stand just to the side of or behind him and watch the faces of the people who sat in front of him. It was amazing to witness the weight of their lives melt away and soften into the incredible joy that one experienced with him. Frowns turned into smiles and tears into laughter. It was the most beautiful thing in the world to see. As I travel around and chant now, I'm reliving that same experience night after night. I feel like I'm sitting there once again, watching the power and sweetness of Maharaj-ji's love wash the sadness from the lives of the people who come to sing. It's exactly the same. I'm watching, and he's doing everything.

In these moments of "temporary sanity," my heart can't contain the gratitude I feel for being able to do what I do. In my wildest dreams, I'd never have been able to imagine a life for myself that had so much grace and so many blessings. My eyes rain a flood of tears, and I find myself sitting in front of Maharaj-ji again, as I used to do when I was with him physically.

I am home again.

Acknowledgments

Thanks go to:

— Patty Gift, who got the ball rolling many bad lunches ago, and for her thoughtful reading;

— Ned Leavitt, my agent, for his dogged determination to get me to get this written and his devotion to the integrity of the manuscript;

— Reid Tracy, president of Hay House, for his patient support;

— Shannon Littrell, Jill Kramer, Christy Salinas, Amy Gingery, Jami Goddess, and all of the folks at Hay House;

— Prema Michau, without whose inspiration, dedication, and hard work this book would never have made it to print;

— Parvati Markus, "private secretary," for her "grace-full" editing;

— Archit Dave, for recording the workshops from which much material was taken;

— Shyama Chapin, for all of the transcriptions;

— Devaki Garin, for the quote permissions;

— Mark Gorman, for a beautiful cover design and invaluable work on the photos;

— Mohan Dada, for his photo seva;

— MC Yogi, for the title of the book;

— Nina Rao, for keeping it *all* together so I can keep chanting.

A SELECTIVE GLOSSARY

Antaryamin—indwelling presence in our hearts.

Ashtavakra Gita—the "Song of Ashtavakra" is a scripture that documents the dialogue between the Perfect Master Ashtavakra and Janaka, the King of Mithila. It teaches that one is already free once one realizes one is free. Ramakrishna, Vivekananda, and Ramana Maharashi often quoted from it.

Avatar—Sanskrit for "descent," is the incarnation of a being from the higher spiritual realms to the lower realm of Earth for a special purpose. There are ten avatars of Vishnu, including Rama and Krishna.

Bhagavad Gita—Sanskrit for "Song of God," the 700 verses that are a part of the Mahabharata. In it, Krishna and Arjuna are conversing on the field of battle prior to the start of the Kurukshetra war. Krishna explains to Arjuna his duties as a warrior and prince and elaborates on Hindu philosophy and how to live life.

Bhajan—an Indian devotional song, a lyrical expression of love for the Divine.

Bhakta—a follower of bhakti, the path of devotion.

Bhav—the human emotions that spring from our state of mind, the outward expressions of our inner state.

Bodhisattva—Sanskrit term for an enlightened being or wisdom-being who is motivated by great compassion. The Bodhisattva Vow is the dedication to the ultimate welfare of other beings, and lasts until all sentient beings are liberated from samsara.

Brahmachari—a celibate. Many brahmacharis are aiming for nirvana through strictly disciplined lifestyles, but the actual meaning is: residing in Brahman, God.

Brahmin—the highest caste in the caste system—originally educators, scholars, and preachers. Brahmin is an anglicized form of the Sanskrit *Brahmana,* which means "he who possesses the knowledge." Also known as the "twice-born."

Chidakasha—The "Sky of the Mind," the subtle and vast space of awareness in which we can experience God, Guru, and Self as one. No distance in time or space can separate the true disciple from the guru.

Danda pranam—full prostration, indicating total surrender to the guru or God.

Darshan—Sanskrit term meaning "sight," as in beholding or having a vision of the divine or being in the presence of a holy person.

Dasya bhav—establishing a near and dear relationship with the Lord in which the devotee behaves like a servant, with his Lord as his master. Hanuman is the ideal servant of God.

Dhobis—those who wash clothes, often in a river or stream. Men frequently do the washing, and women the ironing of the clothes.

Gopis—from Sanskrit, "cowherd girls"—particularly the group of 108 milkmaids who lived in Brindavan and were famed for their unconditional devotion and playful relationship to Krishna during his youth. One gopi in particular, Radha, is especially esteemed as having the highest form of unconditional love for God.

Guru—the one who removes the darkness from our being. From the Sanskrit *Gu*, darkness, and *Ru*, light; literally a preceptor who shows others knowledge (light) and destroys ignorance (darkness).

Gurubhai (Gurubahin)—"brothers" (and sisters) who are devotees of the same guru.

Gyani—a fully enlightened being; a follower of the path of knowledge or self-awareness.

Hanuman—an incarnation of Lord Shiva, who was embodied in the form of a *Varana* (the monkey race) in order to serve Lord Rama (an avatar of Lord Vishnu as the embodiment of dharma, righteousness). Hanuman's amazing exploits are told in the *Ramayana*. The "Hanuman Chalisa" is a hymn composed of 40 verses in praise of Hanuman. (My CD *Flow of Grace* and the accompanying booklet teach how to sing this hymn.)

Japa—a spiritual discipline that involves the repetition of a mantra or Name of God. It may be done while meditating, performing activities, or in a group setting. The word stems from the Sanskrit root *jap,* meaning "to utter in a low voice, repeat internally, mutter." Japa is frequently done on a mala, a string of 108 beads (made from various woods, seeds, or precious stones that carry spiritual vibrations).

Karma—Sanskrit word for the concept of "action" or "deeds"—the entire cycle of cause and effect, wherein the effects of all deeds are viewed as shaping all past, present, and future experiences. Karma is said to be produced through our thoughts, words, actions we perform ourselves, and actions others do under our instructions.

Kirtan—chanting the Divine Name. From Sanskrit, meaning "to repeat." Kirtan walas are the singers/musicians who do kirtan.

Lila (or leela)—Sanskrit, literally means "sport" or "play"—the activities of God and his devotees.

Lord Krishna—an avatar of Lord Vishnu who is the embodiment of love.

Mahabharata—the major Sanskrit epic of ancient India that narrates the Kurukshetra War and the fates of the two great tribes, the Kauravas and the Pandavas. The Bhagavad Gita is one part of this epic poem.

Mahamudra—Sanskrit term literally meaning "great seal" or "great symbol," indicating the authenticity and validity of the experience of the genuine nature of Mind. It is an advanced form of Buddhist meditation practice.

Maharaj-ji—literally, "great king." In this book, it is the honorific that refers to Neem Karoli Baba.

Mantra—a sound, syllable, word, or group of words that are repeated to bring about a spiritual transformation.

Mela—Sanskrit term meaning "gathering" or "meeting." The Kumbh Mela, a spiritual gathering held every 12 years, is the largest gathering in India. In January 2007, more than 70 million people attended the Kumbh Mela in Allahabad over a 45-day period, making it the largest gathering anywhere in the world.

Metta—a Pali word translated as "lovingkindness." The cultivation of metta is a form of meditation in Buddhism, with the object being to love without attachment and to harbor no ill will or hostility toward others. Very specifically, it implies caring for another independent of all self-interest.

Murti—Sanskrit for form or embodiment, the image of God used during worship.

Namasmarana—Sanskrit term for the spiritual practice of remembering the Name of God.

Prasad—literally means "mercy," and refers to anything that has been sanctified/blessed by being offered.

Puja—Sanskrit term for worship or adoration, a rite of worship performed in the home, temple, or shrine to a murti or person, such as the sadguru. The inner purpose is to purify the atmosphere, establish a connection with the inner worlds, and invoke the presence of God or one's guru. Durga puja is a nine-day ceremony in the fall that honors the Goddess.

Qawali—Islamic Sufi songs praising Allah and/or His Prophet Muhammad.

Ramayana—an ancient Sanskrit epic tale attributed to the Hindu sage Valmiki. It literally translates as "Rama's Journey"—the story of Lord Rama; his wife, Sita; brother Lakshman; and devoted monkey servant, Hanuman. The heart of the epic is the chapter "Sundara Kanda," which is the detailed account of Hanuman's adventures. Many versions of the story exist. The one most associated with Maharaj-ji is the *Ramcaritmanas,* written in Hindi by Tulsidas in the 16th century at the height of the bhakti revival.

Rinpoche—from the Tibetan, an honorific given to Masters in Tibetan Buddhism that literally means "precious jewel."

Sadguru (or satguru)—the true guru, an enlightened rishi/saint as distinguished from other forms of gurus, like teachers or parents.

Sadhan—from Sanskrit, "the means to accomplish something"—specifically spiritual practice.

Sadhu—common term for a wandering monk, yogi, or ascetic.

Samadhi—Sanskrit term denoting the higher levels of concentrated meditation. For bhaktis, samadhi is the complete absorption into the object of one's love. *Nirvikalpa samadhi* is the highest nondualistic state of consciousness, pure awareness. *Sahaja samadhi* is the state of staying in nirvikalpa samadhi and yet being fully functional in this world, like Maharaj-ji. *Mahasamadhi,* the "great samadhi," is the term used for the intentional departure from the physical body at death by an enlightened being.

Samsara—Sanskrit term referring to this physical world where ignorance of one's true self binds a person in desire and the perpetual chain of karma and reincarnation.

Samskaras—the seeds of our past actions.

Satsang—the assembly of people who come together to listen to and talk about spiritual teachings. From the Sanskrit *sat*-true, *sanga*-company.

Siddhis—Sanskrit term for spiritual powers or abilities, literally means "a perfection."

Swaha (or svaha)—Sanskrit interjection that ends a mantra or prayer, like "Hail!" Particularly used in fire sacrifices when an offering is made into the fire.

RECOMMENDED READING

In addition to the wonderful books I've cited throughout these pages, I also highly recommend that you check out the books on the next few pages.

— These titles (and many others) are available through the Neem Karoli Baba Ashram in Taos, New Mexico. Please visit: **www.nkbashram.org**:

- *Miracle of Love,* by Ram Dass. Publisher: Hanuman Foundation (1995).

- *Be Here Now,* by Ram Dass. Publisher: Hanuman Foundation (1978).

- *Still Here: Embracing Aging, Changing, and Dying,* by Ram Dass. Publisher: Riverhead Trade (2001).

- *Paths to God: Living the Bhagavad Gita,* by Ram Dass. Publisher: Three Rivers Press (2005).

- *By His Grace: A Devotee's Story,* by Dada Mukerjee.
  Publisher: Hanuman Foundation (1990).

- *The Near and the Dear,* by Dada Mukerjee. Publisher:
  Hanuman Foundation (2000).

- *The Divine Reality of Sri Baba Neeb Karori Ji Maharaj,*
  by Ravi Prakash Pande Rajida. Publisher: Sri Kainchi
  Hanuman Mandir & Ashram (2005).

— These excellent books, in no particular order, are available
through **Amazon.com**:

- *The Yoga of the Bhagavad Gita,* by Sri Krishna Prem.
  Publisher: Morning Light Press (2008).

- *How to Know God: The Yoga Aphorisms of Patanjali,*
  translated by Swami Prabhavananda and Christopher
  Isherwood. Publisher: Vedanta Press (2007).

- *Bhagavad-Gita: The Song of God,* translated by Swami
  Prabhavananda and Christopher Isherwood. Publisher:
  Signet Classics (2002).

- *Lovingkindness: The Revolutionary Art of Happiness,* by
  Sharon Salzberg. Publisher: Shambhala (2008).

- *A Heart as Wide as the World,* by Sharon Salzberg.
  Publisher: Shambhala (1999).

- *Faith: Trusting Your Own Deepest Experience,* by Sharon
  Salzberg. Publisher: Riverhead Trade (2003).

- *Going on Being: Buddhism and the Way of Change,* by Mark Epstein. Publisher: Broadway (2002).

- *Aghora, At the Left Hand of God,* by Robert E. Svoboda. Publisher: Brotherhood of Life (1986).

- *Aghora II: Kundalini,* by Robert E. Svoboda. Publisher: Brotherhood of Life (1993).

- *Aghora III: The Law of Karma,* by Robert E. Svoboda. Publisher: Lotus Press (1997).

- *Great Disciples of the Buddha: Their Lives, Their Works, Their Legacy,* by Nyanaponika Thera and Hellmuth Hecker, edited by Bhikkhu Bodhi. Publisher: Wisdom Publications (2003).

- *The Art of Happiness: A Handbook for Living,* by His Holiness the Dalai Lama and Howard C. Cutler. Publisher: Riverhead Hardcover (1998).

- *Emotional Intelligence: Why It Can Matter More Than IQ,* by Daniel Goleman. Publisher: Bantam (2006).

- *Dark Night of the Soul,* by Saint John of the Cross, translated by Mirabai Starr. Publisher: Riverhead Trade (2003).

- *Shri Ramacharitamanasa, the Holy Lake of the Acts of Rama,* by Tulasidasa, translated by R.C. Prasad. Publisher: South Asia Books (1999).

- *The Life and Teachings of Sai Baba of Shirdi,* by Antonio Rigopoulos. Publisher: State University of New York Press (1993).

- *The Essential Teachings of Ramana Maharshi: A Visual Journey,* by Matthew Greenblatt. Publisher: Inner Directions (2002).

- *Be As You Are: The Teachings of Sri Ramana Maharshi,* edited by David Godman. Publisher: Penguin (1989).

- *Nityananda: In Divine Presence,* by M.U. Hatengdi and Swami Chetanananda. Publisher: Rudra Press (1997).

- *Instructions to the Cook: A Zen Master's Lessons in Living a Life That Matters,* by Bernard Glassman and Rick Fields. Publisher: Harmony/Bell Tower (1997).

LYRICS FOR THE
CHANTS OF A LIFETIME CD

The CD that accompanies this book is different from the CDs I usually record. The chanting that I do is almost always done as a call-and-response practice, with me "calling" and the "response" chanted by whoever has come to sing. When I record a CD, I usually bring a group of folks into the studio to provide the response, but in this case I haven't done that. So *you* have to do the "response." I know, kinda sneaky. This makes you an active participant in the practice of keeping the flow of the Name going.

The real meaning of all these chants is love. All of these Names are doorways into the love that lives within our own hearts, which is who we are when we can let go of thinking we are who we think we are. Chanting will quiet the mind and open the heart, and you can begin to have your own direct experience of a deeper place inside.

You can use this CD as your own meditation practice. (Simple chords for the tracks on the CD are provided in the front and back pages of this book.)

Enjoy!

Track 1—Baba Hanuman-ji

Namo Namo, Namo Namo Anjani Nandanaaya
I bow to Anjani's son, Hanuman

Jay Seeyaa Raam Jay Jay Hanumaan
Hail and praise Sita and Rama, Hail and praise Hanuman

Jaya Bajarangabali Baba Hanuman, Sankata Mochana Kripaa Nidhaan
Hail and praise to the Lightning bolt–bodied Baba Hanuman,
The Destroyer of Suffering and the Abode of Grace.

Jaya Bajarangabali Baba Hanuman, Karunaa Saagara Kripaa Nidhaan
Hail and praise to the Lightning bolt–bodied Baba Hanuman,
The Ocean of Compassion and Abode of Grace.

Jay Jay Jay Hanuman Gosaa-ee, kripaa karahu gurudev Kee Naa-ee
Hail, Hail, Hail Lord Hanuman, Bestow your grace as my Guru

Hare Raama Raama Raama Seetaa Raama Raama Raama
Hare Raama Seetaa Raam

Track 2—Baba Sita Ram

Seetaaraama Seetaaraama Seetaaraama Seetaaraama

Track 3—Mahamantra (Pahari Wala)

Hare Krishna Hare Krishna Krishna Krishna Hare Hare
Hare Raama Hare Raama Raama Raama Hare Hare

Track 4—The Durga Waltz

Hey Maa Durgaa, Hey Maa Durgaa Hey Maa Durgaa

Track 5—Hallelujah Sri Ram Jai Ram

Shree Raam Jay Raam Jay Jay Raam Shree Raam Jay Raam Jay Jay Raam

Seetaa Raam Seetaa Raam Jay Jay Seetaa Raam

ENDNOTES

[1]From *Rumi: The Book of Love: Poems of Ecstasy and Longing,* by Coleman Barks, published by HarperOne.

[2]From *Songs of the Saints of India,* by John Stratton Hawley and Mark Juergensmeyer, published by Oxford University Press.

[3]From *Unseen Rain: Quatrains of Rumi,* by John Moyne and Coleman Barks, published by Threshold Books.

[4]From *Open Secret: Versions of Rumi,* by John Moyne and Coleman Barks, published by Threshold Books.

[5]From *Unseen Rain.*

[6]From *The Spiritual Teaching of Ramana Maharshi,* by Sri Ramanasramam, published by Shambhala Publications, Inc.

[7]From *Japa Yoga: A Comprehensive Treatise on Mantra-Sastra,* by Sri Swami Sivananda, published by Divine Life Society.

[8]From *The Divine Name in the Indian Tradition,* by Shankar Gopal Tulpule, published by Indus Publishing Company.

[9]From *The Interior Castle,* by St. Teresa of Avila and translated by Mirabai Starr, published by Riverhead Trade (an imprint of Penguin Books).

[10]From *Death Must Die,* by Atmananda and Ram Alexander, published by Indica Books.

[11]From *The Rumi Collection,* edited by Kabir Helminski, published by Shambhala Publications, Inc.

[12]From *Mysticism in Medieval India,* by Shankar Gopal Tulpule, published by Harrassowitz.

[13]From *Kabir: The Weaver's Songs,* translated by Vinay Dharwadker, published by Penguin Books India.

[14]From *Sufis, Mystics, and Yogis of India,* by Bankey Behari, published by Bharatiya Vidya Bhavan.

[15]From *Death Must Die.*

[16]From *The Essential Rumi,* by Jalai Al-Din Rumi (translated by Coleman Barks with John Moyne), published by HarperOne.

[17]From *Face to Face with Sri Ramana Maharshi,* edited by Laxmi Narain, published by Sri Ramana Kendram.

[18]Ibid.

[19]From *The Living Flame of Love,* by Saint John of the Cross, published by Cosimo Classics.

[20]From *The Enlightened Heart,* edited by Stephen Mitchell, published by Harper Perennial.

[21]From *Sufis, Mystics, and Yogis of India.*

[22]From *Shri Sai Satcharita: The Life and Teachings of Shirdi Sai Baba;* by Govind Dabholkar, Indira Kher, and Govind Dabholkar; published by Sterling Publishers Pvt. Ltd.

[23]From *Sufis, Mystics, and Yogis of India.*

[24]Ibid.

[25]From *The Enlightened Mind,* edited by Stephen Mitchell, published by Harper Perennial.

[26]From *Rumi: We Are Three: New Rumi Poems,* translated by Coleman Barks, published by Maypop Books.

[27]From *Kabir: Ecstatic Poems,* translated by Robert Bly, published by Beacon Press.

[28]From *Great Swan: Meetings with Ramakrishna,* by Lex Hixon, by Larson Publications.

ᒥᖚ ᒪᓬᒪᒪᒪᓬ ᒪᓬᒣᒪᓬᒪᓬ

— The author thankfully acknowledges Coleman Barks for permission to reprint from the following books:

- *Rumi: The Book of Love: Poems of Ecstasy and Longing,* by Coleman Barks. Publisher: HarperOne (2003). Reprinted by permission of Coleman Barks.

- *Unseen Rain: Quatrains of Rumi,* by John Moyne and Coleman Barks. Publisher: Threshold Books, Battleboro, VT (1986). Reprinted by permission of Coleman Barks.

- *Open Secret: Versions of Rumi,* by John Moyne and Coleman Barks. Publisher: Threshold Books, Battleboro, VT (December 1983). Reprinted by permission of Coleman Barks.

- *The Essential Rumi,* by Jalal Al-Din Rumi, translated by Coleman Barks with John Moyne. HarperOne (June 1995). Reprinted by permission of Coleman Barks.

- *Rumi: We Are Three: New Rumi Translations,* by Coleman Barks. Publisher: Maypop Books (January 1988). Reprinted by permission of Coleman Barks. Mathnawi VI, 831-845.

— The author thankfully acknowledges Stephen Mitchell for permission to reprint from *The Enlightened Heart* and *The Enlightened Mind,* both published by Harper Perennial.

— The author thankfully acknowledges Shambhala Publications, Inc., Boston, MA (**www.shambhala.com**), for the arrangement to reprint from *The Spiritual Teaching of Ramana Maharshi,* copyright 1972 by Sri Ramanasramam.

— The author thankfully acknowledges the Raman Ashram for permission to use quotes from Ramana Maharshi.

— The author thankfully acknowledges The Divine Life Trust Society for permission to quote from *Japa Yoga: A Comprehensive Treatise on Mantra-Sastra,* by Sri Swami Sivananda, published by The Divine Life Trust Society.

— The author thankfully acknowledges Riverhead Books, an imprint of Penguin Group (USA), Inc., for permission to quote from "Fourth Dwelling, Part I," from *The Interior Castle,* by St. Teresa of Avila, translated by Mirabai Starr, copyright 2003 by Mirabai Starr.

— The author thankfully acknowledges Penguin Books India for permission to reprint from *Kabir: The Weaver's Songs,* translated by Vinay Dharwadker, copyright 2003 by Vinay Dharwadker.

— The author thankfully acknowledges Beacon Press, Boston, for permission to reprint from *Kabir: Ecstatic Poems,* by Robert Bly, copyright 2004 by Robert Bly.

— The author thankfully acknowledges Indica Books, Varanasi, India, for permission to reprint from *Death Must Die*, by Atmananda and Ram Alexander.

— Good-faith attempts to reach Bharatiya Vidya Bhavan, India, to obtain permission to reprint from *Sufis, Mystics, and Yogis of India*, by Bankey Behari, were unsuccessful. Anyone with information about this publisher please contact: S. Littrell, Permissions Department, Hay House, Inc., P.O. Box 5100, Carlsbad, CA, 92018.

ABOUT THE AUTHOR

*I*n the winter of 1968, **Krishna Das** met spiritual seeker Ram Dass and was enthralled by the stories of his recent trip to India, where he met the legendary guru Neem Karoli Baba. Soon thereafter, he left behind his dreams of being a rock 'n' roll star and was on his way to India to meet this remarkable Being. In the three years he spent there with Neem Karoli Baba, Krishna Das's heart was drawn to the practice of Bhakti Yoga—the yoga of devotion—and especially to the practice of *kirtan* (chanting the Divine Names).

Krishna Das returned to the United States and, as he continued chanting, developed his signature chanting style, fusing traditional kirtan structure with Western harmonic and rhythmic sensibilities. He travels the world leading call-and-response kirtans and sharing this deep, experiential practice with thousands of people.

More information can be found at: **www.krishnadas.com**

NOTES

NOTES

NOTES

NOTES

NOTES

NOTES

NOTES

NOTES

We hope you enjoyed this Hay House book. If you'd like to receive our online catalog featuring additional information on Hay House books and products, or if you'd like to find out more about the Hay Foundation, please contact:

Hay House, Inc., P.O. Box 5100, Carlsbad, CA 92018-5100

(760) 431-7695 or **(800) 654-5126**
(760) 431-6948 (fax) or **(800) 650-5115 (fax)**
www.hayhouse.com® • **www.hayfoundation.org**

ℐℛ

Published and distributed in Australia by: Hay House Australia Pty. Ltd., 18/36 Ralph St., Alexandria NSW 2015 • *Phone:* 612-9669-4299 • *Fax:* 612-9669-4144 • www.hayhouse.com.au

Published and distributed in the United Kingdom by: Hay House UK, Ltd., 292B Kensal Rd., London W10 5BE • *Phone:* 44-20-8962-1230 • *Fax:* 44-20-8962-1239 • www.hayhouse.co.uk

Published and distributed in the Republic of South Africa by: Hay House SA (Pty), Ltd., P.O. Box 990, Witkoppen 2068 • *Phone/Fax:* 27-11-467-8904 • info@hayhouse.co.za • www.hayhouse.co.za

Published in India by: Hay House Publishers India, Muskaan Complex, Plot No. 3, B-2, Vasant Kunj, New Delhi 110 070 • *Phone:* 91-11-4176-1620 • *Fax:* 91-11-4176-1630 • www.hayhouse.co.in

Distributed in Canada by: Raincoast, 9050 Shaughnessy St., Vancouver, B.C. V6P 6E5 • *Phone:* (604) 323-7100 • *Fax:* (604) 323-2600 • www.raincoast.com

ℐℛ

Take Your Soul on a Vacation

Visit **www.HealYourLife.com®** to regroup, recharge, and reconnect with your own magnificence. Featuring blogs, mind-body-spirit news, and life-changing wisdom from Louise Hay and friends.

Visit **www.HealYourLife.com** today!

HEAL YOUR LIFE ♥

Take Your Soul on a Vacation

Get your daily dose of inspiration today at **www.HealYourLife.com®**. Brimming with all of the necessary elements to ease your mind and educate your soul, this Website will become the foundation from which you'll start each day. This essential site delivers the latest in mind, body, and spirit news and real-time content from your favorite Hay House authors.

Make It Your Home Page Today!

www.HealYourLife.com®

www.hayhouse.com®

Mahāmantra (Pahārī Wāllā)

The Durgā Waltz

Hallelujah Srī Rām Jai Rām